Fools Books

by Robert English

Dedication

This book is dedicated to George Sandford - endless inspiration

Prologue

Do not be misled: "Bad company corrupts good character."

1 Corinthians 15:33-34

Calgary Gazette

Tuesday July 11, 1967

Last evening the police responded to a residential disturbance in the west end of the city. The homeowners, Harry Young, a 43 year old local businessman, and his wife June were awakened shortly after midnight by noises. Mr. Young retrieved a registered handgun from the night table in their second floor master bedroom and proceeded to confront three masked burglars standing beside an open wall safe on the main floor of the house. Before police could arrive, Mr. Young was shot in the leg and his wife shot in the arm. Mr. Young returned fire and killed one of the burglars identified as Philippe Mauson from Montreal. Two robbers escaped. Police have issued arrest warrants for two men; one approximately five feet eight inches, stout, with blond hair between 25 and 30 years old and the other man is described as younger, thin and approximately six feet with dark hair. Both men are considered armed and dangerous. Police requested the public to call with any tips. According to the homeowner, cash and a few pieces of jewelry were taken from a wall safe. ....

Calgary Gazette

Saturday July 15, 1967

Police have apprehended one of the two burglars from an armed robbery that occurred last Monday evening in the west end of the city. Seventeen-year-old Harris Simons of Calgary was arrested in a motel in Cold Lake after a tip from the public. Police took Simons into custody without incident. The second robber is still at large and ....

Calgary Gazette

Wednesday August 23, 1967

Harris Simons, one of two burglars who fled a robbery in West Calgary on July 10 appeared in court yesterday afternoon. Simons pleaded guilty to the lesser charge of aggravated armed robbery. He was sentenced to seven and a half years in federal penitentiary. A second burglar is still at large. ....

Chapter 1

Hamilton was in direct contrast to Dr. Harold Fresher's hometown of Ottawa. The city spun around a large harbour ringed by homes to the west and coal piles to the east. It did not have the tulip-lined streets, the tall historic government buildings or the mid town canal that Canada's capital boasted. However, it did offer the uniqueness of one-way streets that made Hamilton difficult for many to navigate, all except those born and raised there. The city nicknamed 'Steel Town' celebrated its world steel manufacturing leadership by the constant smoke plumes that spiked into the sky above, the tall stacks often depositing fine ash on nearby roofs and cars.

Fresher was in his office having just returned after a relaxing week in Ottawa enjoying Christmas 1988 with his family. After six days of food, food, and more food, he promised himself to eat only salads for the rest of the month. He smiled thinking of the four pairs of socks and two Christmas themed sweaters that his family gave him. He was glad that he got into the habit a few years ago of giving cheques to his nieces and nephews. It made things so much easier and they could spend it anyway they wanted.

The entire time in Ottawa, he thought about Jenn Gallager, a woman he met this past December at Church. She was middle aged, attractive, with dark brown hair and smiling eyes. He sensed there was an immediate connection between them. It had been too long since he felt strongly attracted to a woman, the last time a university girlfriend. He knew that getting to a serious stage may not be in the cards for him and Jenn, but he made a New Year's resolution to seek her out at Church and ask her to dinner. That would be his opportunity to see if she felt the same attraction.

Sitting at his desk enjoying a fresh made Sumatra blend coffee, he stared out the window as a snow-rain mix was making the morning traffic more chaotic than usual. He reflected on the decision he made to leave his teaching post at Royal Military College, start his business, and felt more strongly than ever that he had made the right decision. The diversity of the challenges combined with what he was learning from each case was much better than the usually boring days in class and the stiff shirt receptions every other weekend. Frankly, he was tired of the academia. For him, each case was a jigsaw puzzle and each piece a clue to getting to the end. He remembered something that he heard at university in Sault Ste. Marie; 'solutions aren't hard to find if you have all the clues'.

The first two years in business were more successful than he thought they would be as three fairly large cases and a string of smaller ones built a solid reputation. The income gave him longer-term assurance for his business that included Samid, his assistant, and a nice office on the main floor of one of downtown Hamilton's oldest commercial buildings. The limestone exterior blocks were no doubt from a local quarry and had held up well for the seven decades since the building was erected. He felt comfortable in his office, decked out with an antique desk and leather chair that he spoiled himself with after he was paid for successfully concluding his first case.

It was Tuesday January 3rd; his first day back after the holiday, and Samid scheduled three one-hour appointments for the morning. This was a tighter schedule than he preferred but he knew that the first few days after the holiday would be a bit frantic. As Samid left his office, Fresher smiled seeing Samid wearing the arrow belt buckle he brought back for his assistant when he was on a previous case.

The third appointment was with Mrs. Pamela Cody. She was scheduled for 10:30 a.m. but was a half hour late. Fresher learned long ago that first impressions were more often right than wrong and he took his initial observations as the first indicator of the person. When she did arrive, she was flushed and out of breath signalling Fresher that she must have been late for a reason.

Mrs. Cody was tall, with auburn hair and obviously in good shape. He could tell it was her natural colour. Her eyes were hazel, a colour that he did not often see and she wore no makeup. A dark pantsuit was partially covered by a hooded quilt winter coat and she wore no hat or gloves. He saw a woman that he pegged as honest and no doubt a hard worker. He guessed she was around thirty five. That would make her a dozen years younger than he would be. He felt a strange connection with her, realizing that she had many of the same attributes as Jenn Gallager.

"Hello Mrs. Cody. Let me take your coat and please have a seat. Can I offer you a coffee? It's a Sumatra blend and quite tasty."

"Thank you Dr. Fresher. Yes, that would be nice. I apologize for being late."

"That's all right Mrs. Cody. The first few days after the holidays seem to be more demanding than other times for all of us."

"I should explain. My husband and I own a small delivery company downtown and a last minute employee sickness needed to be dealt with. January is always a busy time of year for the business. Many of our clients are opening after a week or two off and they rely on us to get important documents moving again."

In an attempt to put her at ease, Fresher said, "I understand. I often use delivery companies myself. In fact, I am not sure we would be able to operate effectively without services that you offer. How is the coffee?"

"Excellent Dr. Fresher, it's not often that I have time to actually sit down during the day and enjoy a fresh coffee."

"Mrs. Cody, what can I do for you?"

Pamela Cody paused for a few seconds looking down toward her coffee cup before she started.

"My husband left and I didn't know why."

Fresher could see she was devastated and felt hurt. Her face was beet red and her eyes wet as she dabbed at them with a tissue.

Fresher needed to stop this as soon as possible.

"Mrs. Cody, you should be aware that I don't take on domestic disputes between married couples. I can recommend a few companies that can help you out. They are more skilled at finding or following people and taking pictures in preparation for divorce proceedings."

"Dr. Fresher, this is not a domestic dispute and frankly, I don't think there is another woman involved. There is more, much more that I can tell you that may change your mind. I just don't know where to start."

Samid booked Mrs. Cody for an hour and even though she was late, there was still time before the next appointment and Fresher became somewhat intrigued by her comments that, 'there was much more to her story'.

"Okay, let's hear what you have to say, Mrs. Cody, and please start at the beginning."

"Well, last week....."

Fresher interrupted her. "No Mrs. Cody, the very beginning. I want to know all about your husband. What is he like? What is his background?

What motivates him in life? How did you meet? How has your marriage evolved?"

Over the next twenty minutes, Pamela Cody related the story while Fresher took notes. Her husband, John Cody was born in Calgary in 1951 and orphaned a few months later. He was adopted by a family that he described as dysfunctional, left that home at sixteen and went to the oil fields near Peace River, Alberta. He spent eight years there, but the work eventually became too demanding and the weather too brutal. He moved to Winnipeg in 1975 when he was twenty-four and took a job as a driver for a courier company. She described John as very frugal and independent as a single man. He kept his used car in excellent condition and spotless. Pamela also lived in Winnipeg and was married in1972, but her first husband was killed in an industrial accident before their second anniversary. She went into a shell preferring to read and work rather than party and travel.

In September 1979, Pamela was twenty seven and working as an accounting supervisor at a company where her father was a partner. She never regained interest in men after her first husband died, that was until she met John. It happened one evening when she was out with a few girlfriends bowling. John was in a league playing the same night in the adjacent alley. He was a tall man with well kept trimmed dark brown hair and moustache accenting a much defined face with a square jaw. She was mesmerized by his hazel eyes, the same as hers, which were rare. What really caught her attention was his modest clothing. Most men in those days usually sported polyester checked pants and wildly patterned shirts.

John was one of those who preferred a button down broadcloth shirt and chinos. Other men who approached her displayed a false bravado in hopes of scoring a date, or better yet, a night. John was different. She knew from the first time she saw him that he was not that type of man.

During the evening, both Pamela and John found themselves at the counter ordering a soda pop. When she looked at him, he was almost timid which was an attraction for the widow and he was the polar opposite of many men who had made passes at her in the past few years. She also liked that he did not drink alcohol.

A little later, she saw John head back to the bar for another coke and for some strange reason, she followed, this time smiling and saying hello. They struck up a conversation and things went on from there. Both knew that there was something between them and agreed to meet that weekend for dinner. Pamela was so hoping that all the good things she imagined about him would be realized. They were. The subsequent dates were everything they expected, wanted and needed.

During their engagement, John was very attentive and faithful. He was never late for a date, always opened the door for her, never pressured for sex, and brought her a flower each time they met. Her many girl friends often told her in jest that if Pamela tired of John, they would gladly take him.

They were married in May 1980 and marriage did not change John. He remained mindful of spending except for what she wanted. His love for

Pamela always took first place in his life, each day being a day that many married woman could only dream about. Pamela had found a life and a love that exceeded any life and love that she ever imagined.

Within two years, John was promoted to dispatcher and they started talking about the possibility of starting a delivery company of their own. He did have a college certificate in business that he got through night school while working in the oil fields so understanding business came easy to him. John learned to save as soon as he started to work in Winnipeg and had a nice sum invested. Pamela kept her first husband's life insurance money in treasury bills. With Pamela's accounting skills and John's business interest and desire, they decided to pool their money and take a real leap of faith. In 1983, they relocated to Hamilton and opened up a small delivery service, JP Expediting. Besides better weather than the harsh longer Winnipeg winters, Hamilton was close to Toronto and they felt that there would be some spinoff business. In addition, Hamilton was a lot less expensive than Toronto to set up shop, especially in a downtown location. Being mindful of not getting too far into debt, they leased a small building on Upper Gage, bought three older vans, and hired two drivers. John took care of customer relations and operations including the dispatching while Pamela looked after the marketing and the finance responsibilities. Their focus was on 'small package-on demand' expedited delivery service that quickly became important for lawyers and bailiffs needing to get court documents delivered quickly and real estate agents moving offers between agencies. The business did well for just over five years. Then in mid October of the past year, John, without any warning, left her. She had not heard from him in over three months and was giving up hope of ever seeing him again.

"Mrs. Cody, you implied that he wasn't returning. How do you know that?"

"Dr. Fresher, let me share some things that make me believe that he doesn't intend to come back and that he may be in some kind of trouble."

Pamela described four specific issues that made this much more than a domestic problem between husband and wife. The first was in early October. One evening after work, they got home and there was a voice mail asking for a person named Harris to call Max back. John just passed it off as a wrong number, but he was clearly agitated by the message. He didn't sleep well and his eating dropped off.

Second, a week after the wrong number, she was out October 16th at a Professional Women's Club dinner and when she came home, his clothes were gone. He took all of his toiletries as well as his jewelry that he kept in a small wooden box in his top drawer. The next morning, she checked their joint account and most of their money was gone. He did leave the company money and their joint investments. She continued to run the company the best she could and clung to the hope that John would return soon.

The third was that the couple kept a wall safe in the house in case it was too late for a document to be couriered that day. In the safe was an antique broach that her grandmother gave her just before her first marriage. Her father told her that it was one of the only family heirlooms that existed and that it needed love and protection. John would take it out every year in November and have it cleaned for her. She rarely wore it except for a Christmas dinner that the Professional Women's Club sponsored when husbands were invited. The setting was only ten carat gold, but eight one half carat diamonds in a circle was it's real value. This past Christmas, she was putting it on before the dinner and dropped it. The clasp on the back broke off so she took the broach to a jeweller the next morning for repairs. When she picked up the broach a few days later, the jeweller told her that it may not be worth fixing it again as it was worth no more than fifty dollars. The gold had value, but the stones were fake. She told Fresher that she cried after learning of the fake stones. In shock, she immediately went home and pulled out an appraisal done on the broach the year after they moved to Hamilton. The value was over eight thousand dollars, and probably a lot more now. Nobody except John and her knew the combination to the safe.

The fourth was something that may seem insignificant to anyone but her. John had two old large buttons that he wore on a neck chain when they met. It was a typical chain that also had a crucifix on it. She questioned John about the buttons and he told her that they were keepsakes from his adopted parents. He never took them off until they were married and eventually stored in our wall safe at our home here. The buttons were gone the day he left.

"Mrs. Cody, I am beginning to see why you came to me. Did you talk to the police?"

13

"Yes, I did speak to them but they were reluctant to get involved as they said it was domestic dispute. There wasn't even a chance to tell them about the broach or the telephone message. Once they heard that John took the money and all his clothes, they weren't interested."

"Mrs. Cody, I want to confirm what you said. John took most of your money in the joint account, but not all of it, and he didn't touch any of your combined investments of business money. Is that right?"

"Yes. He took about three quarters of our personal chequing account which was around three thousand dollars."

"Thanks. I also have to ask you this. Could there be anyone else in his life, perhaps a girlfriend?"

"If there was, he certainly covered it up. We were business partners and we saw each other virtually every day from breakfast right through to bedtime. Our days were longer than most given the demands of the business. We knew that sacrifice was what we needed to give if we wanted to make a go of it. We often dreamt about making the business successful, selling it before we were fifty years old, and moving down south. The only free time we afforded each other was Sunday during the day and most Sundays we were too exhausted to do anything except catch up on our physical relationship, if you know what I mean. He went out once a week to bowl and I belonged to the Professional Women's Club of Hamilton, and believe me, they know everything about everybody. The Club knew that he left me within a day of his leaving. I really don't think there was another woman. Dr. Fresher, I need help and I am told you are the best in the business. If money is an issue, please don't worry about that. My father is a successful man in Winnipeg and we spoke yesterday about what I needed to do. He will cover any expenses that I cannot. I took the liberty of bringing a retainer of five thousand dollars hoping that it might compel you to take the case."

Fresher delayed responding for a minute.

"Mrs. Cody, I'll take the case, not just for the money, but I think there is much more to John's leaving than you know. You may not like what I find. I will need the broach, the appraisal that you had done, a recent photo of John, and if you have one, a good photograph of the buttons that he kept in the safe. You mentioned that he had a college business certificate. Do you know where it is?"

"No, I never saw it. I did ask him once about it and he said that after he completed the education part time in Peace River, he lost the certificate."

"Please include anything else you think would be helpful."

"Thank you Dr. Fresher. I will drop everything off this afternoon."

"Before you go, can you tell me anything about John, perhaps habits, idiosyncrasies, likes and dislikes?"

"As I said, John was not a drinker and wasn't out all hours of the night. He had only a few friends, mostly the men he bowled with. He never left a morsel of food on his plate and was partial to good desserts but didn't gain weight due to the pace of our business. He was a very neat and orderly man. I would always have a chuckle as he carefully folded his underwear and socks before putting them into his drawer after they were washed. His shoes were always polished. Perhaps the one thing that is most important is that John held a very special outlook on life that made our marriage uniquely special. He was very diligent in terms of time on the job as we are in a time sensitive business, but in his personal life he preferred to live not in minutes or hours, rather, he lived in moments, positive moments such as happiness, kindness, and tenderness. This was extra special for me as I was usually the recipient of these moments."

"Do you know if he maintained any connection with his family?"

"No. As I mentioned, the family was very dysfunctional and he couldn't wait to leave. As soon as he was old enough, he left for the oil fields."

Pamela Cody was now weeping and Fresher handed her a box of tissue.

"Dr. Fresher, losing my first husband was terrible. I vowed never to feel that way again, but I cannot help it. If it wasn't for my friends at Christmas, I don't think I would have made it through the holiday. Please bring John back to me."

"I'll do my very best. I would like to speak with a couple of your employees and perhaps a few customers if you don't mind. You said he had a few friends. Names and numbers would be appreciated."

"I'll include lists along with the items you asked for. Do whatever you need to Dr. Fresher."

As soon as Pamela Cody left the office, Fresher called Samid to join him.

"Samid, I would like you to find as much information as you can about JP Expediting, their clients, any conflicts that the company experienced, etc. Also, see if you can reschedule the rest of my day."

Chapter 2

Fresher sat at his desk late in the day looking over the material that Pamela Cody dropped off. The broach was finely crafted and the stones looked real. It was the type of jewelry that one would see in old photographs and a fashion style that was slowly making a comeback. The appraisal was in typical jeweller language. It was described having eight E colour, WS2 clarity diamonds, each one half carat, set in a 10K gold setting. Birks Jewellers did the appraisal in 1984. Those folks don't make mistakes, he thought. According to Pamela Cody, the stones must have been replaced within the past five years, kept in the safe at home, and only Pamela and John had access to the broach.

The two pictures of John Cody were eight years apart. In the older picture, he was a tall handsome man with neat dark hair, moustache and rugged facial features, and as Pamela Cody said, hazel eyes. In the more recent picture, he retained the handsome appearance and lean body having avoided the typical post wedding bulge around the middle. Fresher did notice a small spot on his right hand in both photographs. He took out a magnifying glass and looked closer. It was a tattoo with two letters' OK'.

Included was a picture of the buttons that Pamela Cody described but the image was not that clear. There was also a photo of Pamela and John on a beach having a picnic taken a few summers ago. A chain around his neck held the buttons. Again, Fresher needed a magnifying glass. The buttons looked to be about the size of quarters and seemed quite scratched up. He would need a better picture.

****

Samid left the office early to tend to some banking leaving Fresher to close up. Just after six o'clock, Fresher turned the lights off and left through the rear door to the parking lot. As he reached back to lock the door, his foot slipped on a small patch of ice forcing him to push out with his left hand to stop his fall. When his hand hit the doorframe, a protruding nail ripped into his hand. He looked at the cut and shook his head in disgust, as he knew he needed a few stitches.

With his handkerchief wrapped around his hand, he entered the emergency entrance at the hospital. The wait was over an hour but he had no choice. Hungry and just about to look for a vending machine, he heard his name called and was led to a small draped cubicle. Within a few minutes, Fresher heard footsteps coming closer. A nurse pulled the drape back and came in. It was Jenn Gallager.

With a surprised look on her face, Gallager's eyes widened and a smile formed. "Harold what did you do to yourself?"

Tongue-tied and knowing his face was flushed, he replied, "Jenn! I...I...it's you. I grabbed a nail. I mean there was a nail. I mean I slipped."

Gallager's smiled and she gently took Fresher's hand removing the makeshift bandage, "Let me have a look. Oh, that doesn't look too bad. I will let the doctor know that you'll need a couple of stitches. When did you last have a tetanus shot?"

"I can't remember."

"Well, I suspect you will need one."

"A shot, you mean a needle? Where?"

Gallager tried to muffle her laugh. "In the arm Harold."

Fresher's face was the picture of relief.

Still chuckling, Gallager left and returned fifteen minutes later with a needle and small vial.

"Tetanus first Harold. Here let me help you roll up your sleeve."

Harold felt a small poke. Just as she finished, the doctor came in holding a chart.

"Dr. Fresher? Let me have a look. Yes, that looks like a few stitches. Nurse, can you pull out a suture kit please. Dr. Fresher. Are you the same Dr. Fresher that has that private investigation company that I keep hearing about?"

"Yes that would be me. Only good things I hope."

"Yes, only good things. A couple of my general practice clients speak highly of you."

"Thank you Doctor."

Fresher could see Gallager standing at the side smiling.

Two needles froze the area and the doctor quickly closed the wound with fifteen stitches.

"There you go Dr. Fresher. Good as new."

"Thank you Doctor."

"Dr. Fresher, this was a very jagged cut so I put in a few extra stitches. Normally I would suggest seven to eight days before having them removed but in this case up to fourteen days."

The doctor left leaving Jenn to bandage it up.

"I thought you said a few stitches. Fifteen?"

Jenn let out a chuckle.

Fresher stood up and reached for his coat, then turned and asked, "Jenn, do you work this shift all the time?"

"No. We have three nurses off with the flu so I stayed to help the ER. Actually, you are my last patient for today."

Fresher saw his opportunity. "Have you had dinner yet?"

Almost startled, she replied, "No."

"I haven't either. Will you join me? That's the least I can do for receiving your care."

"Give me ten minutes. I'll meet you in the main lobby."

****

The two went to a nearby bistro and spent the better part of an hour and a half finding out about each other. Gallager told him about her abusive marriage and divorce and finding new pleasures in life such as her rewarding Church work and enjoying theatre. Three times throughout dinner Fresher said something that made Jenn laugh and each time she reached over and tapped his arm. She was fascinated by his career change and sat spellbound as he gave her the highlights of his most recent cases. Fresher felt so comfortable with Jenn and she made it clear that she hadn't enjoyed an evening like this for a long, long time.

"Jenn, I started a new case today and will be tied up for a week or so. Would it be okay if I called you as soon as it's over, perhaps theatre and dinner?"

"I would love that Harold."

Outside the restaurant, the night had turned into one of those magical times. The traffic was non-existence and silence filled the air. A light snow was falling and left over Christmas lights added a calming ambiance to the street. Fresher intended to shake her hand but instead, she gave him a quick hug. Gallager turned and walked toward her car. Fresher stood staring at her.

****

Fresher was in his office early the next morning and called Pamela Cody before seven o'clock knowing she would be at her office.

"Mrs. Cody, I have a few of questions if you have a minute."

"Please call me Pamela. Go ahead Dr. Fresher."

"Pamela, call me Harold. I'll start with the buttons. You said the buttons were memories from his adopted family. It seems like a very strange keepsake but I guess we all have our sentimental side. The picture isn't clear but they do look very beat up. Is there something etched on one of them?"

"I looked at them that closely only once. There were some letters and numbers. I asked John once about the letters and numbers but he said that there was no meaning. I know that we have more photos that may be better close ups. I'll try and find them."

"Thank you that would be helpful. Now about the broach. Assuming that John did have the diamonds replaced, when do you think he could have done it?"

"Well, as I told you, the broach was appraised five years ago. I only wore it once a year around Christmas and I never noticed anything different even when I took it to the jeweller last month. I guess the stones could have been replaced anytime in the past five years but I suspect that this happened last year."

"Why do you think that?"

"I would have known if he suddenly came into a lot of money. Harold, I know you have heard this from wives in my situation before, but we did have a loving, open relationship and no secrets. I feel that the diamonds were part of his disappearance. I know that doesn't help much."

"Actually, that makes a lot of sense. Pamela, I noticed in one of the photos that there was a tattoo on his right wrist. I think it reads 'OK'. Do you know where he got it and what it means?"

"John told me that before he stopped drinking, he and a few others from the oil fields got drunk one weekend and they all got 'OK' tattooed in their wrist. It stood for Oil Kings. It was a guy thing I guess."

"That explains why the tattoo looks rough. An amateur in the oil fields trying to earn a few more dollars probably etched it in the skin. Did he have any other tattoos?"

"No."

"Let me shift to another question I have. Did John ever travel alone or without you?"

"Yes he did."

"Can you give me the details?"

"Yes, once a year, in mid September, he and a few of his Peace River buddies went on a fishing trip to Saskatchewan. He was usually gone for six days. This past September, he was gone only three days. He said that he wasn't feeling well, so he came home. The next week or so, he was quieter than usual and I just put if off to his illness. Even the staff mentioned to me that he didn't seem himself. Now that I think of it, he was unusually quiet from when he came home from Saskatchewan until he left.

"You said you had a loving open relationship. Did you not ask him what was wrong?"

"More than once, but he kept deflecting saying he still felt under the weather."

"No other trips?"

"Other than the fishing trip, we really never did anything by ourselves outside of Hamilton."

"Did you know the names of the other men or do you know where exactly in Saskatchewan they went?"

"The only thing he mentioned to me was that there were two other men, Curt and Paul but he never mentioned last names. He flew to Regina to meet his buddies and they would rent a car and take off from there. I know this because I saw his itinerary virtually every year. Harold, we truly enjoyed a loving and secure relationship. I never doubted him and he never doubted me."

"Yes, I understand. Did either one of you have any debts?"

"Nothing of any size. Our house is paid off; we lease our office and have just begun to replace our old vans with newer vehicles. Our fleet is four now. We have some GIC's at the bank for our retirement. Our credit cards are in the company name and I make sure that the balance remains less than five hundred dollars. I just remembered something else. He left all his credit cards in his desk at the office."

"You're telling me that he took three quarters of your chequing account but left all his credit cards?"

"Yes, that's right."

"You mentioned he took around three thousand dollars from your joint account."

"Yes."

"Can you think of anyone who may not have liked John?"

"We have a few competitors, but there is never any animosity. In fact, we often hire each other as subcontractors when business gets too busy for any one of us. As I said, he bowled once a week and there wasn't a person who didn't like him. We didn't have the type of friends who would cause him harm."

"Thank you Pamela. If you think of anything else, please call. I will reconnect with you in a week or so."

"Harold, before you hang up, are you regretting taking this case?"

"Not in the slightest."

****

Fresher paced in his office after the call with Pamela Cody. He was convinced that this wasn't a typical domestic squabble. There were too many factors telling Fresher that John Cody wasn't with another woman and certainly wasn't pulling out with all the money.

Samid arrived and came into his office with a few cheques to sign. He saw the bandage on Fresher's left hand.

"What happened to you?"

"There is an exposed nail on the rear door frame. Slipped on the ice and took a few stitches. Nothing serious. Can you let the building owner know so he can do something about it?"

Within an hour, one of Pamela Cody's drivers dropped off two more photographs of John, both showing the buttons more clearly. Under a magnifying glass, Fresher could now make out the etchings on one of the buttons. The letters and numbers were done very crudely but clear. MK143, WB 28. They were too exact to be meaningless. No doubt, the etching was done several years ago. He wrote the letters and numbers down on a piece of paper.

He made a quick call to Pamela.

"Pamela, its Harold Fresher again."

"Did you get the additional photos?"

"Yes, that is why I am calling. The letters and numbers on the button are very clear, MK143, WB 28. Are you positive that you don't know what they mean?"

"As I said Harold, I have no idea."

Samid came into Fresher's office late in the afternoon to report.

"Dr. Fresher, JP Expediting is a small but highly respected company. I spoke with two employees and three customers, and the feedback was glowing. John's disappearance shocked them all but there is no question that Pamela has picked up the slack with the help of a new dispatcher."

"Thanks Samid. I thought that is what you would find. Can you look at these letters and numbers? Does anything come to mind?"

Samid took the paper and stared at it for half a minute. "No, but perhaps the letters are short forms for something. I'll see what I can find."

Chapter 3

Fresher reviewed his notes. John Cody was very untypical for a man who up and leaves his wife. Most men leaving unexpectedly would have taken all the money, regardless if it was in a joint account, a business account or invested, not to mention the credit cards. It was almost as if he was leaving his wife's life intact. What Cody didn't count on was the broach being dropped and needing repair. Fresher was convinced that Pamela was right; the stones in the broach were replaced in October the same time that Pamela sensed the change in him. The broach seemed like a good place to start.

Fresher knew that it was unlikely that any reputable jeweller would exchange the stones without having the original bill of sale. There were a lot of people looking to make a quick buck, but John Cody didn't seem like the sort to know or associate with them. In Fresher's mind, it meant a jeweller, a diamond merchant or a pawnbroker. Pawnbroker would be the most likely to be involved.

A visit to the Hamilton Police Services was first. Over the course of his first year in business, Fresher developed a good relationship with most of the senior officers on the force. They knew him as a very competent and above board investigator who treated his profession seriously. He wasn't a hard drinker or a liar and avoided many of the easy cases that were left to those only interested in making enough to put food on the table

Fresher understood that the police often reached out to pawnbrokers when they were looking for stolen merchandise. The results were dismal but every once in a while it paid off. It wasn't difficult to have a picture of the broach faxed to all the pawnbrokers in the area with Fresher being the contact should anyone recognize it. The fax made it very clear that the broach was not missing; it was only a request for anyone who may have seen it and a 'finder's fee' was promised. He thought that there would probably be no response. After all, replacing stones wasn't something that went along with legitimacy.

Over the next day and a half Fresher reread his notes planning what he would do next. Would it be a search of the oil fields for some of Cody's history, perhaps tracking down his fishing friends, digging into his background in Winnipeg before they met, or even speaking with his adoptive parents?

Two days later, on Monday January 9th, before Samid made the morning coffee, Fresher was very surprised when he got a call from a pawnbroker in Toronto. The conversation was short and to the point. The pawnbroker saw the broach last fall but wasn't prepared to talk unless in person. Fresher immediately drove to meet the man at his store in Toronto.

The store was in a newer strip mall in the north end. The sign was small and except for the window bars, it was hard to tell it was a pawnshop. As soon as he walked in, a woman behind a long glass counter full of watches and cameras smiled and welcomed him. Odd, he thought, there was no cage that the employees usually sat behind for protection. Fresher did notice several cameras mounted on the wall before a man came out of the back room.

"You must be Dr. Fresher."

"How did you know?"

"My job is to know people."

Fresher assessed the man as a no nonsense guy. "You called about a broach?"

"Yes. I saw it last fall. A man came in asking if I wanted to buy the stones. I told him I wasn't interested and he left."

"That's it?"

"No. He came right back and asked me if I knew of another pawnshop. I knew what he was really asking, 'did I know someone who might want the diamonds'. I suggested Hector's downtown. Everyone in our business knows who specializes in these things."

"Hector's?"

"Yes, and what about the reward?"

Fresher handed one hundred dollars to the man and left.

Fresher found Hector's easily. The store was the classic old time pawnshop with the bars on the windows and door and a large sign hanging over the sidewalk. He smiled when he realized the sign included three brass balls, a very traditional pawn symbol. The window display case that faced the street held a large collection of cameras and electronics. There was even a stained-glass tiffany lamp, not something one normally sees in a pawnshop. Fresher wondered how many of these items would have been stolen. He entered the well-lit store and a buzzer went off. Along the back wall was a wide glass and wood cubicle facing the door. Inside was an unshaven and frumpy middle-aged man behind plexi-glass with a small opening at the bottom and several small holes face high. There was no one else in the store and Fresher approached the man slowly. He knew from experience that there was probably a gun under the counter with a hand resting on it

"Hello. I am Dr. Harold Fresher. I am a private investigator. Can you look at this photo for me?"

"Why?"

Fresher kept his distance and went on to tell the man that he was looking for any information regarding a broach. He accentuated that the police were not involved and they wouldn't receive any information from this visit. Fresher went on to tell the pawnbroker that the broach belonged to a client and it was appraised in 1983 at a value of eight thousand dollars.

Last month it was reappraised and it turned out that the stones were fakes. He had been hired by the owner to find out what happened.

The pawnbroker was silent. Fresher could tell that he was still sizing him up. Then he spoke. "Look pal, I don't know how you got here but you should just turn around and leave."

Fresher decided to bluff. "I could leave, but I have information that you know what I am talking about."

After a minutes silence, the pawnbroker shook his head slightly.

"How do I know you are not a cop?"

"Here. Have a look at my identification."

Fresher approached the window and held up his private investigator credentials. Then he slid a picture of the broach under the opening.

"I may have heard something about it."

"Can you be more specific?"

"What if I did see it? Would I be in some kind of trouble?"

"No. I am not a cop and for what it's worth, I am just like your lawyer, anything I hear is confidential and as I said, I just want to help a woman find out what happened to the real stones from her broach."

Fresher slipped a crisp fifty dollar bill under the glass. That seemed to relax the pawnbroker.

After a long pause, the pawnbroker said, "Okay, I saw the broach."

Fresher knew that there was a lot more. The pawnbroker was still evasive so he repeated that there would be no trouble if the pawnbroker would give him the whole story. He decided he needed to be more firm with the owner.

"Listen, we don't want to waste anymore time. If I brought the cops, you would have been arrested by now. If I was going to try to force the story out of you, I would have brought a gun. So, let's drop the 'what-if' and get to what happened."

There was another long pause before the pawnbroker spoke.

"It'll cost you another hundred."

Fresher slipped five twenty dollar bills under the window.

"I saw the broach a few months ago. Some guy came in and wanted to hawk it. I looked it over and told him I wasn't interested."

Fresher could sense he was holding back. "I just want the truth." Fresher slid another hundred under the glass.

After a very long silence, the pawnbroker opened up.

"Let's say I bought the stones. Let's say that I paid ten thousand and replaced them with fakes. Let's say it was in October last year."

Fresher pulled out a picture of John Cody.

"Is this the man?"

"Yes. He came in and asked if I wanted to buy the stones and if I could replace them with glass. He said he needed cash so we agreed on a price. I told him I could do the work but would need a week to get the right size glass and the cash. He came back a week later but he wasn't alone. There was another guy with him. The guy was about five feet eight or nine had blond hair and a real paunch. Anyway, I did the job in an hour, gave him cash in an envelope and the broach back, and the transaction was completed."

"What did the two men do after that?"

"They left the store and stood out front for a couple of minutes. The tall guy gave the envelope to the short one and they went in separate directions. They didn't shake hands or smile at each other. It was like a payoff. I thought at that time that it may have been a drug deal, but the tall guy didn't give me the impression that he was into that type of thing. Look, this business arrangement was between the tall guy and me. There was nothing wrong with it."

"Ya, ya, I know. Do you still have the stones?"

After a third long pause, "Yup. Tried selling them but reputable jewellers won't touch them and there aren't a lot of folks wanting loose diamonds, especially with a jewellers mark on them. I am planning to have them put in a setting and sell as one piece."

Fresher saw an opportunity. "How much to put them back in the original setting?"

The pawnbroker's eyes widened and he didn't hesitate for more than ten seconds. "Fifteen thousand."

"Fifteen thousand?"

"Hey, I have been out of pocket ten thousand for a few months, plus all the work I did."

"Will another hundred hold them for a couple of days?"

****

Fresher went back to his office and called Pamela Cody. Her first reaction was to ask about her husband.

"I do have some information but first let me tell you what I found out."

Fresher was very cautious and wasn't prepared at this time to introduce the other man with John at the pawnshop into this mystery. Fresher focused on his success finding the real stones. He explained that he found the gems but didn't give too many details about the pawnbroker except to say that John had the stones replaced in October of the past year for a substantial amount and held back that he didn't know what happened to the money. The stones were still with the individual that bought them from John and would be willing to reset them into the broach for fifteen thousand dollars.

Pamela's reaction was swift. "Yes, have them reset. Harold, is there anything else?"

"No Pamela." He lied for her sake.

The next morning, Fresher picked up a bank draft for fifteen thousand and the broach from Pamela Cody. Her father was only too happy to give her the money. Fresher drove to the pawnbroker and as soon as Fresher entered, the pawnbroker put a closed sign on the door and locked it.

"You have the money?"

"Yes." Fresher passed the bank draft and broach to the pawnbroker.

Fresher watched for over two hours as the man put the real gems back in the setting. While this was happening, Fresher noticed that there was a camera mounted in the upper right hand corner that was pointed towards the door.

The pawnbroker handed the broach over to Fresher. The broach looked perfect.

"Any chance that the fifteen thousand would include a look at the store tape the day that the two men came in?"

The pawnbroker smiled and handed him a copy of fourteen inches of the tape.

"I thought you might be asking for this. I pulled it off yesterday after you left. It was from my camera on October 15. I am only giving you the section with the two men. Some of my other customers may not take too kindly that I am giving their pictures to a stranger. Just like you, I am a priest of confidentiality"

"Look, I need to know why you were so cooperative."

"I can smell a chance to make money. Leave it at that."

****

With the broach and the tape in hand, Fresher sat in his car, held the celluloid up to the light and saw what he was looking for. There was clear footage of both John Cody and his friend. On the way back to Hamilton, he made a stop at the local photography shop that he had used several times before. The owner knew exactly what he wanted. Within a half hour there was a clear coloured five by seven still shots of the two men. His next stop would be Pamela Cody.

Pamela Cody was in her office when Fresher walked into JP Expediting. Her reaction was more than Fresher expected. Her hands began to shake and she needed to sit down. Her eyes were staring at her desktop where Fresher placed the broach. Within seconds her hands folded tightly around the broach and she sobbed uncontrollably for a few minutes. She couldn't stop saying, thank you.

"Pamela, I need to apologize for not telling you everything yesterday. I wanted to make sure of my suspicions first. I did manage to get something else along with the broach. It is a picture. Do you know the man with John?"

She looked at the photo for several seconds. "No, I don't recall ever seeing him. When was this picture taken?"

"It was taken October 15th at the location where I found the gems."

"That was the day before John left. Is the other man in the picture part of John's leaving?"

"Yes, I believe he is. Pamela, I have a couple of things that I would like to explore and it may add to my expenses."

"Harold, you have done much more than I hoped. The broach is so important but not as important as getting John back. If you need more than the retainer I gave you, just ask. I still want John back."

"No, I don't need more money at this time and I know John is your first priority. I'll keep you posted. By the way, I suggest you change the combination to the safe before putting the broach back in it."

Fresher was back in his office late afternoon, one mystery solved. With the diamonds back in the broach, he separated some of his thoughts into five key questions.

Was John Cody really sick causing him to shorten his fishing trip?

Were the telephone messages for Harris really the wrong number?

Why did John Cody give the money to another man?

Why didn't John Cody take more money?

How much do the letters and numbers on the button mean to this mystery?

Everything was pointing to John Cody's history. Fresher knew that it wasn't uncommon for young men, especially ones who knew they were adopted or from broken homes to leave as soon as they could and wind up in the oil fields or on deep sea fishing trawlers. They are typically uneducated and looking for a quick fortune. It was even more uncommon for these men to find a respectable life with a loving wife. It was time to look into John Cody's past and Fresher felt he needed to go right back to Cody's adoption.

Chapter 4

The late afternoon flight to Calgary took two hours but the time change had him landing the same time he took off. As soon as he exited the airport, he remembered what he knew from earlier trips there. Winter in Alberta was a real winter. There were still businessmen walking around with Stetsons and a lot of women wore either heavy wool or fur coats. He was happy that he brought along his parka and fleece lined boots.

After checking into his hotel, he enjoyed a western steak dinner. Fresher savoured every bite of the medium rare rib eye. He knew he could order this in any steakhouse in the east, but somehow it tasted better in Cattle Country. Enjoying an after dinner coffee, he looked ahead at the challenge that he would have digging into John Cody's past, especially researching the adoption process. Ideally, he planned to be in Calgary for only two days, hoping to get the information he needed quickly and return to Hamilton as soon as possible. Back in his hotel room, he was exhausted from meeting with the pawnbroker, then returning the broach to Pamela Cody, then the flight. He was in bed by nine o'clock.

Fresher had asked Samid to track down an old friend Misha Hossam, and request her to meet Fresher over breakfast. He knew Misha would make time for him as he had been one of her referees when she presented her thesis. He followed all of the Masters students whom he helped over the years and was delighted that Misha was now Associate Professor of Child Advocacy at the University of Calgary. Fresher hoped that she could help him through the minefield of Children's Aid and the adoption agency.

As soon as Fresher entered the hotel restaurant, he saw her sitting at a table by the window. She smiled and rose from the chair and they had a brief embrace before they both sat down.

"Misha, it's great to see you again. How is the family?"

"Harold, they are happy and healthy. Both daughters are in high school and doing well and my husband is still with the mining company. Things are good."

"I'm glad for you Misha. What's it been, fifteen or sixteen years?"

"At least. I heard you left RMC and have a private practice in Hamilton. How is that going?"

"Yes, it was a major decision but one that has turned out well, in fact better than expected so far. I have an office downtown, and you spoke to my assistant Samid. I really lucked out in the first year with cases that paid very, very well. It's a different town than Ottawa where I would have been up against a telephone directory full of investigators whereas in Hamilton, it's a much smaller community. We even get some of the overflow business from Toronto. How about you Misha?"

"I was tenured three years ago and recently offered full professorship but I am not sure that the extra work is worth the trouble. I have a couple of weeks to decide. The Dean wants his team set before the final exams begin. What do you think? You had full professorship at RMC."

"It may be more work but there are a lot of perks including an increase in your social life. Your daughters are old enough to need less mothering. I recall your drive and my sense is that you should take it."

"You're probably right. Thanks. Anyone in your life Harold?"

"No, but there is a 'person of interest' so to speak." Fresher wanted to change the subject. "Listen Misha, thanks for meeting me so quickly."

"I always have time for a great friend. Harold, Samid mentioned on the phone that you needed some help regarding a boy in foster care here in Calgary. How old is he?"

"I think I need to explain. He is over thirty and was in the system quite a few years ago."

"What can I do?"

"The short version is a woman's husband left her and for me the story starts here. I believe he was born in Calgary in 1951. I know that his name is John Cody. He was orphaned within a few months after birth and subsequently put into the foster care system."

"Harold, are you taking domestic dispute cases?"

"No Misha, this is quite complicated. I am convinced it is not a typical husband-wife fight and separation. After it wraps up, I will give you a call and fill you in. I am not sure where it will take me, but I have a strong instinct that the husband may be in trouble. The case involves some stolen gems and a mystery man seen with the husband the day before he left his wife. Right now, I need to focus on anything that may help so I am starting here."

Misha Hossam sat back absorbing what Fresher told her. Her eyes stared at Fresher as if to say, 'I need to be careful.' She began by explaining that the Children's Aid Society applies very stringent controls on access of information and that it would not be an easy task to get anything from them. Given that he was an orphaned child suggested that the parents were probably killed leaving the boy behind. If that was the case, the best place to begin would be the newspaper. It was the type of story that newspapers would jump all over. Every reader loves these heart tug stories. If the newspaper didn't pan out, Hossam asked Fresher to call her. They finished breakfast chatting about old times, got up to leave and hugged briefly.

"Misha, I can't thank you enough for meeting me and giving me advice."

****

Fresher was off to the Calgary Gazette to look at the archives. Having the year was a big bonus. Starting January 1, he painstakingly leafed through each issue. By close of business that day, he was only at the end of February so he went back to his hotel and extended his stay.

The next morning, he was at the newspaper as soon as it opened. By ten o'clock, his eyes were sore and he was only starting May. He decided to grab a coffee before he continued. As he got up from the table and tossed the May 3rd issue down, there it was. The page two headline read, 'Baby Boy Abandoned on Church Steps'. As Misha predicted, the story was long and detailed. It was full of adjectives embellishing a story that would normally be a hundred words but now was a quarter of a page. The article reported that a baby boy approximately two months old was found outside St. Leonard's Catholic Church. A priest witnessed the abandonment and also recognized the mother. He knew she lived close by and the police quickly located and questioned her. According to the story, the mother said she just couldn't cope as a young mother with a newborn. As she was a minor, she could not be identified and the baby was put in the care of the Children's Aid Society until a foster home was found. No charges were filed.

Excited, Fresher made a call to Misha.

"I found the article I was looking for."

"Let me guess, a baby survived a car accident. Both parents were killed."

"Not even close. Listen to this. On May 2nd, 1951, a baby boy was found abandoned at a church. The mother's story is sad. The outcome of the situation was that the baby was put in the care of the Children's Aid Society until a foster home could be found. The mother was a minor and couldn't be identified. I cannot be sure that it is my guy. I may have a dead end but I have a gut feeling about this."

"Harold, didn't you tell me that the man that went missing in Hamilton was John Cody?"

"Yes."

"Well that might be a strong lead."

Misha Hossam went on to explain that in all likelihood, the name Cody was the name of the family that adopted him since a minor abandoned him within a month or so after birth. It was doubtful that the child would have an original birth certificate with the biological parent's names on it. The probability is that the only birth certificate would have been in the name Cody. Looking for a family by the name Cody would be a starting point.

"That's a very good idea Misha. I should have thought of that but my mind is so full of questions that I just didn't get to it."

****

There were four families by the name of Cody in the Calgary phone book and four calls asking about a son named John ended with four rejections. None of the families had a family member by the name John. He was back to square one.

Somewhat dejected, Fresher made another call. "Misha, I struck out. No John Cody's. I guess that the family moved. They could be anywhere. The parents may even be dead. I guess I'll head back to Hamilton."

There was a long pause before Misha spoke. "Harold, are you here to the end of the day?"

"Yes, why?"

"Leave it with me. I think I may be able to help."

Late afternoon, Fresher was packing when the phone rang. It was Misha.

"I have something that you will be interested in Harold. Can you meet me at the university coffee shop in the next hour?"

Fresher was excited, immediately left his room, and hailed a taxi. Misha was waiting at a corner table with two cups of coffee and as he sat down, she pushed one cup toward him.

"Thanks Misha. This will taste good after the cold walk across campus."

Misha Hossam sat straight faced. "Harold, we'll need to be quiet."

She explained that she spoke to a friend who was retired from Children's Aid. As a favour to her, he was able to find out that there was no family in the system called Cody. She gave him the date May 2nd, 1951 as a second clue. This turned out to be what he needed. That day, a baby was left abandoned at a church and subsequently adopted out. The family that took the boy was called Simons.

"Harold, I suspect that he was born with one name but in so many of these cases, the birth is never registered. When he was adopted out, his new parents would have registered him and he would have been given their last name, in this case Simons. Any information on the birth mother would be locked and can only be given legally to the adopted child and only if the birth mother approves. How the name John Cody comes in to this, is any one's guess. Perhaps John Cody isn't the Simons boy or perhaps Simons just changed his name."

"Yes, looks like this may be another dead end unless the name Simons can be traced. Thanks Misha."

"I know that you will do all you can for the wife of the missing man, but please don't implicate me or my friend. If the authorities even sensed a leak, all hell would break loose."

"Misha, the best part of my job is that I have immunity when it comes to revealing sources, and in this case, you have my personal assurance that my sources will never be revealed. Besides, I don't want to lose you as a friend."

Fresher returned to his hotel and immediately postponed his flight. It was too late to be calling people so he decided to wait until the next morning. Starting at 9:00 a.m., he called each Simons listed in the phone book. Being very careful, he heeded what Misha said, so when a person answered the phone, he explained only that he was looking for a missing person from Hamilton by the name of Simons. The missing person, an adult man now, was originally from Calgary. He provided a very brief description including that he told his wife the missing husband was adopted. There would be no mention of the name John Cody.

On the fifth call, he struck pay dirt. The woman who answered was only too happy to help with any information that she could provide about her son Harris Simons. She was very accommodating and invited Fresher to her house to chat.

****

"Mrs. Simons, we spoke briefly on the phone and I want to thank you for seeing me. As I said, my name is Dr. Harold Fresher and I am helping a lady in Hamilton who is trying to find her husband."

"You're a doctor?" He could smell cigarette smoke and booze on her breath.

"Yes, but not the medical type. It's just a post graduate degree designation."

Mrs. Simons looked at Fresher with an awkward look on her face not having the slightest idea what he had just said.

Fresher remembered that John Cody described his childhood to Pamela as being part of a dysfunctional family. Looking around, he understood what he meant. No two pieces of furniture matched. There were dirty dishes a few days old on the counter, and the floors were badly worn. The house hadn't been cleaned in quite a few weeks. Several family photos were on the walls, some with cracked glass. In the middle of the table was an ashtray with at least twenty butts in it and a half-full gin bottle beside it. Mrs. Simons was clearly a few drinks into a new day well before noon. An old mangy dog slept in the corner. Fresher thought that if this was any example of the environment that John Cody grew up in, no wonder he thought it was dysfunctional.

"Doctor, can I pour you a drink?"

"No, thank you. It's a bit early for me. Can we talk about the boy that you adopted?"

Mrs. Simons refilled her glass and sat in a well worn chair preparing to answer Fresher's questions. After each sip from her glass, she became more and more communicative. She went on to explain that together with her now deceased husband, they adopted three children in the early 1950's. Her husband was a long haul truck driver and for every adoption, the government gave them money and continued financial support with monthly baby bonus cheques. The children kept her company while he was driving and the extra money helped to sustain the household. She vividly remembered the boy they adopted in early May 1951. The Simons initially took him in as a foster child then adopted him and named him Harris after her maiden name. She pulled out a few pictures of him as a baby. Harris knew that he was adopted and for the first ten or eleven years, he developed as any typical boy that age, but when he was twelve, he began to get into trouble. At first, it was school where he lost interest, then the fighting, some petty theft, and as he got into his teens, drinking and more serious trouble with the police. This carried on until he was sixteen. The problems came to a head when he was arrested for car theft. As the car wasn't damaged, Mr. Simons convinced the car's owner and the police to release Harris to their custody until a date in juvenile court would be set. That custody lasted a week, a week of arguments, fits of temper and damage to furniture and doors. The court gave Harris a reprimand for the car theft largely because the owner said he didn't want a young man to endure a conviction when there was no real damage.

Her son's behaviour didn't improve after the court case and as a result Mr. Simons was very leery of leaving Mrs. Simons and the other children alone with Harris so he gave him an ultimatum, shape up or ship out. Harris left the house in June 1967 and didn't return. He took money as well as valuables from the house. Mrs. Simons jokingly made reference to two large buttons from a baby sweater that he also took.

Fresher perked up when he heard about the buttons and became more attentive to Mrs. Simons' story.

The next time the Simons heard from him was a month later when he was arrested for robbery and attempted murder in Calgary. Harris called from jail asking to be bailed out but the Simon's were still upset with what happened at home and in reality, they couldn't afford the bail as it was set high because of the seriousness of the crime.

The time in court went by very quickly. Mr. and Mrs. Simons attended the proceedings but according to Mrs. Simons, the boy would not acknowledge them, obviously mad that they hadn't bailed him out. They were surprised to find out that Harris was being tried as an adult because the homeowner and his wife were wounded and the accomplice shot to death. A third person of the three man robbery team was still at large. Harris refused to provide the name of the missing accomplice. Even though Harris did not have or use the gun, he was implicated. The original charge of attempted murder was reduced to aggravated armed robbery on a plea bargain by the court appointed defender and a sentence of seven and a half years in the penitentiary was handed down. After court, they never heard or saw Harris again.

Fresher needed to confirm that John Cody was Harris Simons, but was reluctant to show her a picture that he kept with him. If he did and she recognized him, he could be jeopardizing John Cody's future with Pamela. Fresher couldn't trust Mrs. Simons especially now that she had consumed another drink so he took the opposite approach.

"Mrs. Simons, would you have any pictures of Harris around the time he left home?"

Mrs. Simons rose and in slightly unsteady steps, went to another room and reappeared a few minutes later with a shoebox full of old photos. As she leafed through them, she gave a short commentary for each one. A few brought tears and others laughs. Fresher persevered through the photos of her deceased husband, the other two adopted children, friends, relatives and family pets. The visit was becoming a painful experience that Fresher put down as just part of his job.

"Yes, here is a photo of Harris when he was fifteen. He was always tall for his age, and had that thick dark hair. As he matured, he took on a very rugged look. A lot of the girls liked those hazel eyes. There were more than a few times we caught him trying to sneak a girl into the house late at night. He had so much promise as a young boy but threw it all away."

Fresher quickly came to a very uncomfortable realization, not only was John Cody really Harris Simons but Pamela Cody had no idea that his time in Peace River was really spent in prison for armed robbery. Fresher sat stunned. This must be kept confidential until Fresher could understand why and how John Cody did what he did.

There was more that Fresher needed and he returned to the buttons.

"You mentioned two large buttons."

"Yes, the buttons were from a blue baby sweater that he was wearing when Children's Aid brought him to us. We wanted our children to have as much of their past as possible and Harris' only past was that sweater. He loved the sweater and kept it in his room in a box under his bed. I found the box on his bed the day he took off. The sweater was there but the two large buttons were gone. The only secret we kept from him was the fact that his mother abandoned him. Harris never asked and we never told him of the circumstance. He would probably find this out later in his life as the story was in the newspaper."

"Was there anything special about the buttons, any reason why he would take them?"

"No. They were those typical large buttons that would be on any infant's sweater, you know the ones that wouldn't fit in a baby's mouth."

"Did Harris have any tattoos?"

"No. My husband would have been very mad if any of the kids got a tattoo. That was a strict rule in the house. No Tattoos."

"Well, Mrs. Simons, you have been very helpful. I appreciate your time."

Mrs. Simons lifted her glass and drained it before rising to escort Fresher to the door.

"Oh, Dr. Fresher, I did keep the press clippings on Harris' arrest and conviction. Would you like to see them?"

Fresher couldn't wait to leave but wanted to get as much as she would offer. "Yes, please."

Mrs. Simons brought out all the press clippings including the details of the night of the robbery, his capture and his incarceration. While Fresher sifted through the material, Mrs. Simons poured another drink and lit another cigarette.

The stack of articles was small and Fresher went through them quickly dwelling on one in particular.

'Harris Simons, one of two burglars who fled a robbery in West Calgary on July 11 appeared in court yesterday afternoon. Simons pleaded guilty to the lesser charge of aggravated armed robbery and waived trial. He was sentenced to seven and a half years in federal penitentiary. A second robber, approximately five feet eight inches, stout and blond hair remains at large. A third robber was shot and killed by the home owner."

Finally out the door, the fresh air was a welcome relief. He waited only a few minutes for the taxi to arrive and as he sat in the back on the way back to the hotel, he digested all the information that Mrs. Simons gave him including the button mystery. The story was reaching epic proportions involving an obvious name change, lies, crime and punishment and stealing from his wife to pay some mystery man, a man with the same description as one of the robbery accomplices. That description also matched the picture of the man who accompanied John Cody into the pawnshop and took the money afterwards. So, after many years, the short man reappears in Cody's life with some pressure on Cody to get ten thousand dollars. John Cody returns early from Saskatchewan in September and is uncharacteristically quiet until he took off. The timing of everything was all too coincidental. However, to Fresher, John Cody worked too hard and too long cleaning up his life to abandon everything he built since leaving prison. There must be more and he was going to find out what it was.

Chapter 5

It was noon and he had changed his flight to eight that night. This gave him time to do two things. The first was to call Misha to answer a key question for Fresher.

"Hello Misha."

"Hi Harold, how did you make out?"

Fresher started by thanking her and telling her that the boy who was adopted in 1951 was the missing man in Hamilton. He told her a bit about the boy leaving at sixteen and running into trouble and of the transition that the boy, now a man, made to become a respectable husband and business owner.

"Misha, you mentioned to me that the names of birth mothers are locked and only a child can get the information. Is there any legal way that this information can be obtained, perhaps a court order?"

"No. It's been tried with no success. The only way is by a child eighteen or older. The child must produce the adopted family's information that matches what is in the Children's Aid file. It is a long complicated process."

"Thanks Misha, I'll be in touch."

****

The second thing he needed to do was leave early for the airport and take a side trip to the Calgary Police Department to speak to Deputy Chief Paul Parker. Parker had been an outstanding student and was in Fresher's first graduating class at RMC and decided to go into policing after graduation. Parker was surprised to see Fresher standing at the door.

"Dr. Fresher, what a pleasant surprise. What brings you to Calgary?"

"I'm working a case."

"Yes, I heard that you left RMC and opened up a practice in Hamilton. How's that going?"

"Very well, in fact, better that I hoped originally."

Fresher gave Parker a few details of the cases he worked on so far and took some pride in the fact that they had all been solved.

"Paul, I see you have done well."

"Yes. Timing is everything. Turns out that there were a few retirements and I was the right person in the right place at the right time."

"That's great Paul."

"You said you were working a case?"

Fresher told Parker that he took a case of a man in Hamilton, John Cody. Cody left his wife and there were some very unusual circumstances.

"Dr. Fresher, are you taking domestic cases? I remember you telling the class more than once that the problems between husband and wife need to be solved between husband and wife and if they can't, get counselling."

"No Paul, it isn't that simple at all. I originally thought that it was domestic, but there is a changed identity and theft involved. The police in Hamilton pushed this off as a marriage dispute but I feel strongly that there is much more to the situation. The story starts here in Calgary."

"You always said to start at the beginning. I am sensing that you might be in my office to understand a few things. What can I do for you?"

Fresher smiled.

"Still as sharp as ever. Yes, I was hoping you could help".

Fresher went on to ask information about a man called Harris Simons arrested in July 15, 1967 for armed robbery. He would have been sixteen and because he was sentenced as an adult, he went to prison. He was originally from Calgary. Parker left the room returning five minutes later with a file folder.

"Here it is Dr. Fresher. Simons was part of a three-man team that broke into the home and opened a small wall safe July 11, 1967 in Calgary. The husband and wife were at home and heard noises downstairs. The husband retrieved a licensed handgun from the night table, confronted the three men and exchanged fire with one of the robbers. The husband and wife were both wounded but survived. One of the three robbers, Philippe Mauson from Montreal, was shot and killed by the homeowner. Mauson was thirty two with a long record of assault and break and enter. According to the homeowners, all three wore facemasks, but they were able to give a good description of the two that took off. The first was approximately six feet with dark hair and the other was described as approximately five feet eight inches, stout and with blond hair. The police got a tip from a trucker who heard the descriptions on his radio and Simons was found in a motel in Cold Lake two hundred miles north east of Edmonton. Simons gave up without any struggle. In court, he pleaded guilty to aggravated armed robbery and was sentenced to seven and a half years in the Edmonton Institution. Keep in mind that he was originally charged with attempted murder. The prosecution didn't care if Simons used a gun or not, or whether if he even did the shooting, it was tagged as attempted murder. The other man in the crew was never caught and Simons wouldn't tell them who he was, so Simons paid the price. Simons served his full sentence of seven and a half years. There was a supplementary warrant for him issued a week after his release, but it was for failing to check in with a parole officer. Even though he served his full sentence, it was still mandatory to check in once then be on the way. These warrants are filed in ninety days of issue and are forgotten. As far as we know, he hasn't turned up anywhere yet."

"Paul, what was taken in the robbery?'

"According to the homeowner, six hundred dollars in cash and two diamond rings."

"What can you tell me about the homeowners?"

"Interesting family the Young's, Harry and June. They own a string of convenience stores here in Alberta. Anyone that reads newspapers and magazines knows that the Young's are one of those good news stories. They arrived as refugees from Laos just after World War 2. They were relocated to Calgary where they rebuilt their lives and found success."

"Paul, do you have the mug shot of Simons in that file?

"Yes, here it is. It was taken the day he was returned to Calgary by the RCMP that picked him up in Cold Lake."

"Can I have a copy?"

"Sure."

"Is there a list of Simons' possessions at the time of arrest?"

"Yes. In addition to shoes, socks, shirt, pants, a belt, a coat, seventy dollars, a wallet and comb, there were two large buttons. Some guys have some strange stuff when they are nabbed. There was no firearm. He would have been given all of this back when he was released."

"Paul, thank you so much. This has been very helpful. I'll treat to dinner next time I'm here in Calgary. I need to catch a plane."

"I don't think so Harold. The snow has cancelled all flights. The way it is coming down you're here for at least another day."

Fresher finally boarded his flight Sunday mid afternoon and by the time he landed then drove to Hamilton, it was evening so he went home, ate and got a good night's sleep.

****

Fresher was anxious to get back into his office and sat at his desk early Monday looking at two pictures of Harris Simons, the one from his stepmother and the other from his arrest. It was more confirmation that he was John Cody. In the picture, both hands were shown. No tattoo. In all likelihood, he got the tattoo in jail. What it meant was still unknown. He was positive it didn't stand for Oil Kings as it was pretty clear that he was never in the oil fields as he told Pamela. In addition, he had the two buttons when arrested. Why he kept them would need to be answered. Perhaps the bigger question was how between his release and meeting Pamela, a span of four years, Harris Simons was no more and John Cody was born. How he pulled that off was a real mystery to Fresher. Even after the change from Harris to Cody and the several years since his release from prison, someone had tracked him down.

Fresher waited until ten o'clock to make a telephone call to the Edmonton Institution. It wasn't easy to get through to the Warden and Fresher had to reintroduce himself to three layers of administration before the prison secretary told him to hold. Three minutes later, a deep, tired voice said, "Dr. Fresher, Dr. Harold Fresher from RMC?"

"Yes Sir that would be me."

"What does RMC want with me?"

"Sir, I am not with RMC anymore. I am now a private investigator in Hamilton, Ontario."

"A private investigator? Well, I have heard a lot about you as a teacher from a few of my guards. What can I do for a teacher turned PI?"

"Thank you for those kind words Warden. I was hoping to get some information about an inmate that has been out for a few years."

Fresher explained it involved a prisoner that was paroled in 1975. His name was Harris Simons and he had a tattoo on his left hand - OK.

The Warden laughed slightly and related to Fresher that the tattoo was a pass card in the jail.

"A pass card?"

The Warden explained that a pass card was expensive and was an identification that Simons wasn't to be touched. He did something extraordinary and in his case, the Warden offered that it was probably because Simons hadn't given up his partner and he took the wrap for his accomplice. Also, although he was only sixteen, to the other inmates, this was a demonstration he had shown that he was strong and loyal. It was one of the unwritten codes in prison. The Warden was aware that when he was released he never checked in with his parole officer and a warrant was issued. As far as the Warden knew, the warrant expired and Simons was gone.

"What kind of a prisoner was he?"

"I was Deputy Warden at the time and remember him very well. Simons was quiet compared to most. You have to appreciate that it is difficult living in general population in one of the oldest prisons in Canada. The inmates come from a variety of cultural backgrounds and cannot always bunk with someone who they want in the same cell. The constant fighting and complaining was hard on the guards so everyone knew the good ones and the bad ones. When Simons wasn't working in the laundry, he was in the library. He was never in any trouble. In fact, Simons fast tracked a college diploma. Usually it takes four to five years to get a diploma, but he did his in less than three years, and he got it in business, which was more difficult than philosophy, or sociology that others opted for. He also had a special interest in the war in Korea. Can you believe that? A teenage con interested in a war that happened decades ago. His file notes that he was adopted as a child and he spent that last couple of years writing to the Adoption Council of Alberta, probably trying to find his birth mother. We can't open any of the letters going out, only the ones coming in for obvious reasons. Besides the responses from the Council, he corresponded with a pen pal, so to speak. The inmates call them pen pals, but most of them are very lonely women hoping to meet, rehabilitate, and marry some loser."

"You wouldn't happen to have any information of the pen pal, would you?"

"His file said her name was Janice R. Cody."

Cody. The name hit Fresher right between the eyes. It all came together. Janice Cody must have been John's mother. John Cody was a smart young man. Those letters to the Alberta Government were to exercise his right to knowing who his birth mother was. He turned eighteen in jail and still had lots of time to find her and work out his plan. He tracked her down while in jail and she must have prepared everything to give back to him his original identity and disappear as soon as he was paroled.

"Warden, is there anything else you can tell me about Simons?"

"Well, I remember a very unusual incident when he was scheduled to be released. The union for the guards was in a position to strike the week after Simons was to be released. The Attorney General made a decision to release any prisoner in good standing within seven days of the potential strike. So because of this, Simons was sent out four days before his original date."

"Warden, I would like to send you a picture by fax. Simons is one of the men in the picture. I was hoping that you might be able to help me identify the other man."

Later that day, Fresher received a call from the Warden. The man in the picture with Simons was Max Levitch a lifetime criminal who was in and out of jails across the country. He was originally from Toronto. Most recently he was arrested in March 1984 and served three and a half years in British Columbia for assault. According to his file, he wasn't a model prisoner and served full term plus a few months until his release in August of last year.

Chapter 6

Fresher weighed the two options he was facing. Would he try to track down Max Levitch or locate Cody's mother? The answer came quickly; it would be Cody's mother first.

"Samid, I need to find a woman named Janice R. Cody. The only information I have is that she lived in Calgary over a dozen years ago. I don't know if she is still there or married, or dead. It will be like looking for a needle in a haystack, but I suspect that if John Cody found her once, she may know where he is now. I'm going to have another look through my notes to see if I missed something."

An hour later Samid came into Fresher's office. With a wide smile, he said, "I thought you said it would be like looking for a needle in a haystack? Well, there is a J.R. Cody in Regina."

"Regina, Saskatchewan?"

"None other."

"Did you get a number for her?"

While he waited for Samid to make the call, he thought John Cody's fishing trip to Saskatchewan was too coincidental considering his mother could be living there.

"May I speak to Janice Cody please?"

"Yes. I'm Janice Cody."

"My name is Dr. Harold Fresher from Hamilton, Ontario. I am calling on behalf of Pamela Cody, the wife of John Cody.

There was a long pause. Fresher could sense something from the pause and the breathing.

"Dr. Fresher. Can I have your telephone number? I will call you back."

After a very long ten minutes wondering and hoping that Janice Cody would call, Fresher's phone rang.

"Dr. Fresher, I needed to make sure that you were who you said you were. I had a friend in Hamilton look you up in the phone book and she told me that you are a private investigator. Has something happened to John?"

Fresher could hear the anxiety and concern in her voice but decided to address the issue head on. "Mrs. Cody, John is missing and his wife is quite concerned."

"It's Ms. Cody. Please tell me more about John gone missing. I thought something may be wrong because he always called at Christmas but not this past year."

"Ms. Cody, I would prefer to come to Regina and speak to you in person."

"When will you be here?"

"Tomorrow."

"Dr. Fresher, please do not mention me to John's wife. I will explain when you get here."

****

Fresher was at home packing that evening thinking that he never realized how much time he would spend on airplanes when he left RMC to go into private practice. With the suitcase waiting at the front door, he felt the stitches in his hand and remembered that they needed to come out soon. It was still a few days away but he thought he would use this as an excuse to talk to her.

After the second ring, Jenn answered the phone.

"Hello."

"Hi Jenn, its Harold."

"Harold. Are you finished with that case?"

"No. It's a bit more complicated that I originally thought, probably a few more days. Listen, I called about removing the stitches."

"Well, it hasn't been fourteen days yet so I suggest a few more days. Better to leave a day or two longer than risk the wound opening up again. That was a pretty nasty gash and the palm is an active part of the body and you need to make sure it's fully healed."

"That's what I thought. Thanks Jenn. I'll connect with you as soon as I get this wrapped up. Remember we agreed to another dinner."

"I am so looking forward to it. Good luck Harold."

Fresher sat back encouraged by Gallager's response to the dinner comment hoping that the Cody case would be solved soon so he could see her again.

****

Fresher wore his parka to Regina and he was glad he did. The winter prairie wind was bitter and blowing snow that felt like knife blades on the cheek. Even the heater in the taxi wasn't able to keep out the chill. The trip from the airport to Ms. Cody's was twenty minutes and gave Fresher ample time to revisit his plan to speak with her. He felt that he had some of the answers he needed but wanted her to confirm his thoughts.

Janice Cody was waiting for Fresher in her apartment but wouldn't take the safety latch off until he produced photo ID and his licence. Satisfied, she let Fresher in and took his coat. Fresher noticed that she was nervous and was questioning Fresher about her son and daughter-in-law before he sat down. Fresher just smiled and sat down.

"Oh, I forgot my manners. Dr. Fresher, would you like a cup of coffee?"

"Yes, please."

She brought two coffees into the front room and sat in a chair across from Fresher.

"Ms Cody, I know you are anxious, but perhaps we can start with some questions that will help me."

Janice Cody nodded her head in approval.

"When was the last time you spoke with John?"

Janice Cody's hands started to shake slightly and her voice quivered as she responded.

"It was September last year when he came for his annual visit. He left a couple of days earlier than usual. I sensed something wasn't right with him. His monthly letter didn't come after he left. As I mentioned on the telephone, he always calls at Christmas but not this year."

"What did you two do on his September visits?"

Janice Cody spent a half hour reminiscing and relating the times they spent together. There were quiet dinners, going to a show or two, driving into the country and even a trip to the zoo. As Fresher let her continue speaking, she began to become more relaxed.

Fresher was very careful not to cause more concern for Janice Cody than she was already experiencing. The conversation needed to be more about what she would say, rather than what information he could share. He gave her just enough for her to know that Fresher knew the facts about Cody's transition back to his birth name and enough empathy to hopefully get the information he needed.

"Ms. Cody, we both know that John Cody from Hamilton, married to Pamela Cody, is your son. I believe that you were instrumental in reverting to his birth name that helped him disappear after his early release from prison. I am not here to expose any role you may have had in that and frankly, there isn't anything wrong with helping your adult child. As I said, I am working for his wife in Hamilton and hopefully the safe return of John."

Tears welled up in Janice Cody's eyes.

"What do you need to know?"

"Start at the beginning. Anything could help."

She spent the next hour telling Fresher the entire story. She was pregnant at fifteen and the father took off before she gave birth leaving her in a one-room basement apartment. She kept John for a few weeks, but the landlord threw her out complaining about the incessant crying of the baby. She had no choice but to abandon the boy at a Church. Before surrendering him, she registered his birth and picked up his birth certificate a few days after he was placed in foster care. She kept it. Janice Cody lost track of him quickly when he went into the Children's Aid system. She regretted giving him up every day and never gave up hope that she would one day be reunited with her son.

That day came twenty two years later. In February 1973, she started to receive letters from a man named Harris Simons in Edmonton Institution. He claimed that he was her son. She was leery and thought that the first two letters were just pranks and ignored them. In the third letter, Simons described a blue baby sweater with two large buttons that he wore when Children's' Aid delivered him to the Simons house. That letter stunned her. No one except her, the agency and the adopting family could have known about the sweater. Before she could respond, she received a fourth letter. Included was a picture of him. She remembers collapsing in her chair clutching the picture and crying. There was no doubt in her mind. He had the dark hair that began to come out as a two month old, and his eyes were hazel just like hers. He also inherited the rugged features of his fifteen year old father. She knew then that Harris Simons was her son John Cody. She immediately wrote back asking if she could visit but he said no. It would be too dangerous for her and he would explain once he was released. There was however something that he needed her to do. They corresponded for over a year that gave her time to apply for a social insurance card for him that she told authorities was lost. The birth certificate and the signature of a professional was all she needed. A few months before his scheduled release, the plan was in place including her relocation to Regina and renting a two bedroom apartment. A week before his release, she received a call from John telling her that his release was advanced four days.

The day before he was released from custody, she drove to Edmonton staying in a motel. She wasn't about to chance being late. At ten the next morning, she was at the prison gate standing beside her car. As her son walked through the wire mesh doors between armed guards, tears rolled down her cheeks. She vividly remembers his first word to her. 'Mom'. They embraced for several seconds before getting into the car and heading off to Regina. On the drive back to Regina, he pulled out the two large buttons. She didn't need to see them to know that he was her son. She saw that in his eyes. On the long nine hour drive, he gave his mother the complete story about the crime and jail and the reason he felt she would be in danger if she visited him. It was the same danger that he felt he would be in if he stayed in Alberta. That danger was from one of the other robbers who didn't get caught and concerned that he might go to the police with information. He told her about the book he stole but lied telling her the accomplice took the book. She questioned him about the tattoo on his hand and he laughed it off as a prison memento. They finished the ride on a high note by John telling his mother he had finished high school in prison and had earned a college certificate in business administration.

Janice Cody told Fresher that the next three months were the happiest in her life. She got to know her son as a loving, honest man who showed everyone the highest level of respect. He was not overly talkative, but when he did say something, it was meaningful.

His birth certificate and social insurance card were all he needed to start a new life but without experience, there was not a lot of business oriented job opportunities in Regina. John got his driver's licence and worked part time construction to help pay his way, but he wanted a career, so he made a decision to relocate. Janice Cody wasn't happy but knew that he needed to get his life going. As she drove him to the bus station, he promised to stay in touch and she believed him.

****

Janice Cody continued. In Winnipeg, there were not a lot of jobs for people with no experience, but a delivery company took a chance on him as a driver and part time dispatcher. He secured a nice but small apartment, purchased a two year old car and put his past far behind.

Through telephone calls and letters over the next few months, she knew that he had begun his new life. She was so very pleased that he did not slide into a life of crime. Once a year he would take a few days in the fall and visit her. She knew he very seldom dated and was very surprised that he called telling her about Pamela. Janice Cody was shocked when he told her they were married and wondered why she wasn't invited. John made it clear that he could not risk any of his past coming forward now. He told her that his wife did not know anything about Harris Simons, the crime, or prison. To Pamela, he was from a broken home and spent a few years in Peace River working. He promised his mother that he would tell his wife soon. That was okay with Janice Cody. She loved her son and would take anything he could offer her in terms of being that son. In her mind, his rehabilitation, education, and success far outweighed the truth.

The next thing she knew, they moved to Hamilton to start a business. He wrote her every month with an update on his life and set up a post office box for her to return letters. He also continued his annual visit to Regina that she eagerly awaited.

Janice Cody began to cry.

"I'm sorry Ms. Cody; I didn't mean to upset you."

"No, no, it's not that. During his last visit he told me that he was going to tell Pamela everything so we could all be one happy family."

Fresher pulled out the picture of John with the buttons on the neck chain.

"Dr. Fresher, those are the same buttons, I am sure. A week before I had John, I went to the second hand shop and bought a blue sweater for one dollar. The buttons were so big. I loved that sweater. It was so soft and in very good condition. It was what I left him in. As I mentioned earlier, it was his description of those buttons in the prison letters that peaked my interest. They are obviously a big part of his life."

"Did you have a good look at them after he left prison?"

"Yes, why?"

"There were some letters and numbers etched on them. I was wondering if you knew what they meant."

"I saw what I thought were scratches, but that's all I know."

"Please look at this other picture. Do you know the man with John?"

"No."

"Does the name Max Levitch ring a bell?"

"No. Dr. Fresher and I am concerned that something in John's past may have caught up with him. As I said, he left early last September and he wasn't himself. I thought it may the business, or even some problem with his wife. I know that he worked extremely hard to change his life when he was released from prison and I hope that nothing has disrupted that. Do you have any idea of where he is?"

"No, I don't and in my business, you need to be thorough and not jump to any conclusions. If something from his past has caught up with him, as you suggest, I'll do my best to find out what that is. Ms. Cody, you have been very helpful. I appreciate the time. If I find anything out, I will make sure you know."

Fresher extended his hand, but Janice Cody stepped towards him and hugged him firmly.

"Please find my son."

****

On the flight back to Hamilton that afternoon, Fresher knew his next move was to find Max Levitch, but where to start. He knew he was in British Columbia in August when released from prison, then with Cody in Toronto in mid October. Somehow, between those two dates, Levitch found Cody. That wasn't much to go on.

Chapter 7

The next morning Fresher arrived in the office a little later than usual and could smell coffee as soon as he opened the door.

"Good morning Samid."

"Good morning Dr. Fresher. Mrs. Cody is in your office waiting for you. I gave her a cup of coffee."

This wasn't what he was expecting. He was not ready for this and his mind went into overdrive trying to figure out what he would tell her.

"Hello Pamela. I assume you are here to get an update on the investigation."

She jumped up from her chair. "No, Harold. I have some news for you."

Relived but confused, Fresher responded, "I hope it's good news."

"John called me last night."

Fresher stared at Pamela Cody.

"He called you? Where was he?"

"I don't know. He wouldn't say. I tried several times to find out but he wouldn't budge telling me that it was for my own safety."

She went on to tell Fresher that the conversation was no more than four or five minutes long and John was very upset, crying a few times. He told her he was so sorry for what he was putting her through and that he wasn't sure if he would ever be home.

Fresher dwelled on the phrase, 'would ever be home'. This sounded serious.

Pamela went on to tell Fresher that John said there was some history that he hadn't shared with her and that it would be best unsaid. He apologized for taking the money and promised to get it back to her someday. She told him she knew about the diamonds but they were now back in the setting. He cried again but didn't ask how. She told him about hiring Dr. Harold Fresher to find out why he left and where he may be, but he was adamant that Fresher would never find him. He closed the discussion telling her that he loved her and would always love her. Before she could respond, he hung up.

"Harold, do you know what he was talking about when he said that 'there was some history that he hadn't shared and that it would be best unsaid'?"

"Pamela, I have some information but I would prefer to confirm before I pass it on."

"Harold, I think that I deserve to hear what you found out."

Fresher thought quickly and decided to give Pamela Cody information that should satisfy her but keep certain details confidential for now. He related that he was trying to track down John's birth mother. Fresher avoided any hint that Cody was once Harris Simons and served time in jail. That might be too much for her right now. He told Pamela that it appeared that the diamonds were used to pay a person named Max Levitch. He didn't know why.

"Pamela, I am in the process of trying to locate this Levitch person. I believe that he is the person with the information I need to find John. Give me a few more days."

After Pamela Cody left his office, he poured a cup of coffee and returned to his plan to try and find Levitch through information in arrest reports. He would head over to his friends at the Hamilton Police Service and see if the central Canada database contained old addresses for Levitch. That would be a start. He put his cup down and went to leave. Just as he got to the door, Samid called out. There was an urgent call for him.

Fresher went back into his office and picked up the phone.

"Dr. Fresher. How can I help you?"

"This is John Cody."

As the call to Pamela Cody wasn't surprise enough, John was on the phone. Fresher sat down and tried to catch his breath. He knew that this might be the only chance he would have to speak with Cody if he was in serious trouble. He decided the best approach was to let Cody take the lead in the conversation.

"John, I am all ears."

Cody started by telling Fresher that he knew Pamela hired him. He suspected that it was Fresher who found the diamonds and arranged for them to be reset in the broach. He thanked Fresher. Cody also told him that he spoke to his mother that morning and knew that Fresher discovered the truth about the birth certificate and social insurance number, and that the fishing trips in September were actually reunions with his birth mother.

"Dr. Fresher, please don't tell Pamela about my prison time. That would destroy her."

"John, there is a lot more than your prison time that she should know and something you need to tell her, not me."

"I appreciate that, but I don't think that we will ever see each other again."

As the conversation continued, Fresher could sense Cody relaxing a bit more.

"John, let's take it one step at a time. Is there any chance we could meet? I know that you are in trouble and if we can take care of that, you could return to your life."

There was a long pause. "Dr. Fresher, you have no idea what kind of trouble I am in. It could cost lives and the last thing I want is Pamela or my mother caught in the middle. It would take a miracle to get me out of this mess."

The line went dead. Fresher sat for several minutes regretting he couldn't get John Cody to agree to meet.

He headed for the door once again when Samid called out. "Dr. Fresher, it's the same man calling.

"John?"

"Dr. Fresher, you are right. I am tired of all this and it's time to have it come to an end. Can you come to me? I don't have a lot of money left."

"Where are you?"

"I am in Halifax. I needed to get away and this is as far away as my money would take me. I am in a boarding house on Quinnpool. There is a pancake place near the big park on Spring Garden Road."

"I know the place. Give me some time to get organized. I will see you there tomorrow around eight in the morning. I have your picture from Pamela so I'll find you."

Chapter 8

Fresher spent a month in Halifax when he was researching for his PhD and fell in love with the city known for its unique culture, warm people and the laid back approach to life. It offered something for everyone. He particularly enjoyed the waterfront where he could walk and grab a beer at the Lower Deck after a tough day studying, but that was then and this was now. There would be no time for socializing. Getting John Cody out of his mess promised to take all of Fresher's time and talent.

It was winter and the usual number of visitors was typically down. It didn't help that the weather between November and March was a wild mix of rain, freezing rain, snow, all delivered with on-shore winds off the Atlantic Ocean. Today it was wet snow that melted soon after it hit the ground.

The pancake restaurant was only half full, mostly students. Fresher remembered the aroma of bacon and syrup that rushed to greet each customer as they walked through the front door. A scan of the restaurant and it was easy to pick out John Cody. He sat in a corner booth with his back to the wall. As Fresher approached, he could tell that Cody hadn't slept a lot, blinking and moving his head from side to side taking in all the faces.

"Hello John. I'm Harold Fresher." He reached out and shook Cody's hand.

"Thank you for coming Dr. Fresher."

"Please call me Harold."

As soon as Fresher sat down, a waitress came over with a menu in one hand and a pot of coffee in the other. Fresher nodded and she filled the cup in front of him and topped up Cody's cup.

When the waitress was out of earshot, Cody spoke.

"I wanted to thank you for being so discrete with Pamela. If she knew what I did and served time in jail, she would be heartbroken and I couldn't bear losing her love, even if I left. You know that I spent all my time after prison working to establish a good, honest life. Meeting and marrying Pamela was way beyond my dreams and I feel so ashamed that it has all come to this."

"John' I'm here to help you. Tell me the whole story"

"I am not sure where to start."

"John, we can skip the time you spent in the Simons home. Let's start with the robbery and go on from there."

Over the next hour, John Cody filled in many of the blanks for Fresher, as well as adding a lot of new information. John Cody, then Harris Simons, left home and met a man named Max Levitch in a bar in downtown

Calgary. Levitch was full of bravado with a get rich quick plan. John was young and naive and listened with great interest. Levitch, a labourer, was working for a contractor doing a home renovation in a good part of the city. The work included installing a series of security cameras inside and outside the home. Levitch set up the camera in the client's home office and was in another room testing the installation. Just then, the homeowner went into the office and slid a picture on the wall exposing a wall safe. Levitch was able to watch remotely and wrote down the combination. He also saw a stack of money and some jewelry. Levitch's idea was to break in, open the safe and make off with the money and jewelry. A third man, Philippe Mauson would come along. The break in was easy, but something woke the owner and his wife. Just as the safe was opened and Levitch's hand inside, the homeowner was at the doorway to the office with a gun. Levitch pulled his hand out of the safe and all of the contents wound up on the floor. Cody grabbed whatever he could, including a small notebook. What they didn't know was that Mauson had a gun and the shooting started. Levitch and John ran out the door and separated immediately. John hopped on the first bus which happened to be destined for Edmonton. A second bus took him to Cold Lake. On the bus, he did an inventory of his haul. There was about $90 in cash and a small black notebook that was in another language. The only thing he could read was the dates February and April 1951 and two English names that he couldn't remember. He checked into a motel in Cold Lake. On the television, the news ran the story of the robbery. He found out that Mauson was killed and the homeowner and his wife, June and Harry Young were wounded. Money and jewelry were stolen. There was no mention of the book. Cody looked more closely at the notebook in his motel room. Besides what he read on the bus, everything looked to be Chinese. What he couldn't understand then was why this information would be in the safe, obviously important to Young. His instinct told him to hide the book. It could turn out to be valuable if he was caught. He wrapped the book in a plastic bag that lined the waste basket in his room and when it got dark, he went for a short walk up the highway and found a place to bury the book. He etched one of his keepsake buttons to make sure he could remember where it was. MK143 was for mile marker 143 and WB 28 stood for west to birch tree 28 steps.

"John, the etched letters and numbers were a real mystery. Thanks for clearing that up. By the way, you said you had only ninety dollars and the book. The police report said six hundred dollars and two rings. Where did the rest of the money and the rings go?"

"I guess Levitch scooped the rest of the money and the rings".

"Look John, let's move over to my hotel room that I reserved where we can continue this conversation. It will be more private and safer."

At the hotel, Fresher ordered a pot of coffee and sweet rolls from room service. Cody was well into his second cup quickly and devoured three of the rolls.

"John, would you like me to order some real food?"

"Maybe later."

Cody was now very relaxed with Fresher and the major clue was about to unfold. He told Fresher that last September, he went to Regina to see his mother. They spent the morning together and were going to a local restaurant for lunch. When they walked in, just by the worst coincidence, Levitch was sitting alone in a booth eating a sandwich. They both recognized each other and after Cody's mother sat down, Cody excused himself to go to the washroom. Levitch followed shortly after. The conversation was quick and terse. They made arrangements to meet that evening in a pub nearby.

After dinner that evening, Cody told his mother he was going for a walk and went off to meet Levitch. The conversation was disjointed but Cody was able to make sense of Max Levitch's information. Young, the homeowner who they robbed was a very wealthy man. It was a long time since the robbery, twenty three years, but Young tracked Levitch down because of Levitch's stupidity in jail. The first few weeks of his last incarceration in British Columbia, Levitch told another inmate about the robbery in Calgary. Levitch figured that since the robbery at the Young's was so long ago, it was forgotten. The information eventually got to Young. As soon as Levitch left jail, two men picked him up. He was roughed up a bit but not enough to leave lasting scars. They wanted to know where Simons was. Young was very mad when he heard that Simons was released four days early and disappeared. Young told Levitch that his wife saw Simons pick up the book when he was scooping money off the floor and found out that the book wasn't part of Simons' belongings when arrested. Young thought Simons must have it or discarded or hid it but wasn't about to chance that the book would reappear, so he paid for Simons' pass card in the prison.

Fresher interrupted. "Yes John, I heard all about the pass card and heard all about the early release."

Cody told Fresher that he found out very quickly that the OK tattoo that he was given the first week in jail would keep him safe and thought that Levitch arranged for it as payment for not ratting him out. He was surprised to learn that Young paid to keep him safe and now knew that the book was valuable.

Levitch told Cody that Young offered him ten thousand if he could find Simons.. Levitch wanted no part of this and fled to Regina hoping to get a job in the potash mines.

As Cody got up to leave, Levitch pulled him back down and explained that if Cody gave him the ten thousand, he would get lost and stay lost. Cody quickly determined that he had no option so he agreed to the deal and also decided to run, specifically to get and keep Young away from Pamela.

Fresher sat for a minute digesting the story.

"Well John, I can see why you are on the run. That book seems to be at the centre of all of this. Can you repeat what you saw in the book?"

Cody provided the same information as he had before, this time adding that there was reference to the Korean War.

"John, is that why you were so interested in the war when you were in prison?"

"Harold, you certainly did your research."

Fresher could see that Cody was impressed and knew that it added more confidence in his wife's choice of private detectives.

"Do you know if you can trust Levitch?"

"Yes I know that I cannot trust him."

Chapter 9

It was pretty clear to Fresher that John Cody was in much more serious trouble than he anticipated. Even if he could hide, it was probable that Young would eventually find him. If Young hadn't given up in over twenty years, he wouldn't give up now. It was likely that the protectors in prison were able to pass along information about Cody, things like the mail coming in from a stranger named Janice Cody and the correspondence to the Alberta Government. It was only a matter of time that he would be found. Yes, John Cody was right; whatever was in the book from the robbery was more valuable than Cody realized when he scooped it up from the floor.

"John, I can't promise you that I can get you out of this mess, but at least I can try. It is important that we retrieve the book and try to understand the importance of the contents. You need to trust me. I want to go to Cold Lake and come back here with the book if it's still there. You need to stay put. Levitch found you by fluke and I am sure that Young has eyes everywhere. I will extend this room for a few days and leave you enough cash to tide you over, and John, promise me no more calls to your wife or your mother."

"I promise."

Fresher called the airline and booked a seat on a flight to Edmonton leaving late afternoon. With a couple of hours to spare, Fresher ordered lunch for three to the room and Cody ate two of them. During lunch Cody related that the Korean War connection with the book intrigued him and hence the research in prison. As the book was in a safe in Calgary and he saw the date 1951, he suspected that whatever was in the book related to the Princess Patricia's Canadian Light Infantry that trained outside Calgary. He researched as much as he could including the critical battles that the PPCLI engaged in while fighting in Korea. Without the book and its translation, he couldn't go much further.

As they finished lunch, Fresher asked Cody if he ever had any stitches.

"Quite a few actually. In prison I worked in metal stamping and that stuff is sharp."

"Did you ever take your own stitches out?"

"All the time. Why?"

"Well, I have a few stitches in my left hand and I was wondering if you could snip them and remove them before I leave. My nurse told me that they should come out about now"

"That's the least I can do. Do you have a first aid kit?"

"Yes, I have a small case I carry in my luggage."

Cody finished the snipping and renewal within a few minutes. He then put on a small dab of antiseptic cream and covered the scar with a large band aid.

"There you go, as good as new. Listen Harold, I can't tell you how much better I feel knowing you're on our side. Good luck."

'Our side'. Fresher heard that loud and clear. John had not given up on returning to Pamela.

****

Fresher was about to take his third flight on this case and costs were adding up so at the airport he called Samid.

"Samid, I am waiting to board a plane for Edmonton. It's a long story. I'll fill you in later. The retainer that Pamela Cody gave me, is it in the bank?"

"Yes Harold. It cleared a few days ago."

"Have you done any accounting update on what this case has cost so far?"

"As a matter of fact, I have. Including overhead, you have $1800 left."

"Thanks. I'll give you a call when I am leaving Edmonton. And by the way, if Pamela Cody calls, tell her I'm looking into a lead and will call personally in a few days."

Fresher's flight to Edmonton was uneventful and it gave him time to reflect on how complicated life can be when something is hidden from a spouse. On the other hand, there are secrets that need not be known. Either way, he reminded himself that as a single man, he was no expert in these matters. The thought brought Jenn Gallager to mind. He reached over with his right hand and touched the band aid that Cody put over the stitch less palm. That scar would be a constant reminder of Jenn. It was a good scar, he thought.

****

It was winter and driving to Cold Lake would take over three hours. He acquiesced to his common sense and rented an SUV with four wheel drive. As he left the city limits of Edmonton heading north east, the roads were snow covered. Even though he picked up two hours in the change of time zones, night came early in the north at this time of year. He arrived at Cold Lake in the darkness and the motel wasn't hard to miss. It was in the centre of town and featured the only neon sign in the area. Fresher knew that this must have been the same motel that John Cody stayed in.

A typical northern Canada single story restaurant was beside a motel. How convenient, he thought. The drive was exhausting and he was not in the mood for a big dinner. A sandwich and coffee would suffice.

After checking in at the motel, he walked quickly to the restaurant for dinner. His original thought of a sandwich soon disappeared as he read the chalk board special, meatloaf. He couldn't remember the last time he had meatloaf, his mother's best dish. No sandwich tonight, he thought – meatloaf.

A few locals as well as truckers were scattered about the room sitting at checkered cloth covered tables. It surprised Fresher to see such a nice touch so far out of the big city. The waitress, a woman in her fifties, was pleasant but overly inquisitive. Who was he, where was he from, what was he doing in Cold Lake. Fresher told her that he was with Canadian National Railway and was to inspect for loose tracks the next day. That kept her at bay. It was easy to see how a stranger like John Cody would have caught interest and with a description on the radio and television, people were only too happy to help the authorities.

The meatloaf was one of the best he ever ate made even better by creamy mash potatoes and very tasty gravy. It wasn't until he complimented the waitress on the meal that he found out it was deer meat.

The walk to his room was short, but he could feel that the temperature dropped substantially in the last hour. The sky was clear but snow was forecasted for the next day. Fresher got a good night's sleep in the cleanest air he breathed for several years. The serenity of the town was interrupted only by the odd truck heading to ice roads over frozen lakes picking up and delivering to remote towns and reserves.

The next morning, he felt famished and put it down to the crisp air. After a hearty breakfast of wonderfully cooked eggs over easy and moose sausage and more questions from the same waitress, he went back to the motel office and checked out just as snow started to fall. His vehicle was now warmed up and he left to drive a short distance up the highway to mile marker 143. He pulled over and put his four way flashers on. The railway track was about forty feet west of the road.

He looked directly west through increasing snow and saw a single white birch tree. Most of the branches had rotted and fallen from the harsh winter winds and only the bark peeling off the trunk remained. That was fortunate he thought as so many years had passed since John buried his treasure. Starting at the mile marker, he stepped off twenty eight paces. There near the base of the tree, under a foot of snow, was a flat rock frozen to the ground. After kicking it several times, it broke free. He lifted it up and just as Cody told him, there was a plastic wrapped book. Without inspecting the wrapper, he quickly put it in his pocket, got in the car, made a u-turn and started south on the highway. As he drove past the restaurant, the waitress was peering through the window and gave him a smiling wave.

With the snow intensifying, he needed to concentrate on his drive back to the airport and would leave the book until he was on the plane. Fresher turned on the radio and over the dull hum of country and western music he spent the three hour drive back to Edmonton reviewing the case in its entirety. There were a lot of characters, a lot of time that spanned over two decades, lies and deceit. There was even a life turned around and a much grounded love between man and wife. He could only hope that the book would be John Cody's salvation so he could return to a normal life, a life that he worked so hard to create and sustain.

Fresher was just in time to touch base with Samid before boarding his return flight to Halifax. There was nothing urgent requiring his attention and Janice Cody hadn't called. Good, he thought.

The plane was only half full so after takeoff, many of the passengers who were beside others moved to have more room or to get a window seat. Fresher took advantage as well and relocated to a seat with no one near him. The stewardess came through with coffee and tea and Fresher was pleasantly surprised that there was a Sumatra blend. After the first sip, he sat back and pulled out the plastic wrapped book. The book was in surprisingly good condition considering the years it lay partially exposed to the elements. It was four inch square with hard black front and back covers. There were about thirty lined pages inside, most of them with something on them. Fresher couldn't read the book as it was written in an oriental language, perhaps Chinese he thought. Throughout the book, there were some words that John Cody told him he recognized including the Princess Patricia's Canadian Light Infantry, Korea, and dates that looked to be February and April 1951. On the inside back cover were two names - Jason Oliver and Stanley Ward. He had no luck with anything else in the book. He would need to have the information interpreted as soon as he got to Halifax.

As he was closing the book he noticed that the inside cover liner was peeling off at the corner. Fresher couldn't resist picking at it and after a couple of tugs he saw a small piece of patterned cloth underneath, no doubt material used to give the cover some thickness. He looked at the flat cloth, red with small gold dots and rather than put it back, he put it in his pocket returning his attention to the contents of the book.

****

Back at the hotel in Halifax, John Cody was very anxious.

"Did you get it Harold? Was it still there?"

"Yes, John. Here it is. Frankly, I am surprised it is in such good shape. I flipped through it on the plane but can't make anything out of it except for what you already told me. Have a look."

"Yes, this is the book. Harold, it looks like the inside back cover has been damaged, probably the weather."

"No John. The liner was peeling back and I just helped it along."

"Harold, what should we do now that we have the book?"

"Did you have a chance to research the two names on the inside back cover while you were in prison?"

"No. As I mentioned, I forgot the names."

"Does Jason Oliver or Stanley Ward ring a bell? They are mentioned in the book."

"No."

"Well, we can't read the book, so I think I will visit an acquaintance at Dalhousie University tomorrow morning. I met Dr. Chad Elliot on a previous case who should be able to help. Want to come along?"

****

Although it was Saturday, the university was buzzing with activity as the second semester was about to begin the following Monday. Most administrative staff and all the teachers' assistants were busy making sure forms were ready and lessons were planned.

They had a quick breakfast and made their way to Dalhousie, on the way stopping to have all the pages of the book photocopied. Fresher then put the original along with a note in an envelope and mailed it to his office. The note read, 'Samid, put this in the office safe'.

At the university's administration office, just as Fresher remembered, Dr. Chad Elliot was sitting at his desk looking as officious as ever. As soon as Fresher walked in, Elliot got up and walked over to greet the two men.

"Dr. Fresher. It is good to see you again. What brings you back, and on a Saturday no less?"

"Dr. Elliot, this is my assistant John Cody. I was hoping that you could direct us to an Asian language specialist who might be able to help translate something for us."

"Yes, we do have several language specialists. Most are post grad students working as Professor Assistants, you know, trying to eke out a bit of extra income. Is there a specific language?"

"It's Asian. I think it may be Chinese."

"If you go across the campus to Killam Library, our teaching assistants are busy readying for Monday. They will all be there today."

At Killam Library, a few eager students were already engaged in various things from reading massive journals, to researching on microfiche, to having quiet discussions. The Librarian was just getting to her desk with a cup of morning tea. The name plate on her desk said, 'Mrs. Henry'.

"Mrs. Henry, I am Dr. Harold Fresher and this is my assistant Mr. Cody. Dr. Elliot in Administration suggested I come here to see if we could get some help with translation. I think it is an Asian language, perhaps it's Chinese."

Fresher showed her a copy of the page of the book. Without any hesitation, she smiled and agreed it was Chinese then pointed to a young lady sitting at a lamp lit long table on the other side of the library.

"Her name is Carol Lee; she should be able to assist you."

Fresher and Cody approached the young female student.

"Excuse me Ms. Lee, my name is Dr. Harold Fresher and this is my assistant Mr. Cody. Dr. Elliot in Administration sent us here in the hope that you could help us translate a small book that is involved in a challenge we have on our hands. Would you mind having a look at it? We are prepared to pay for your services."

Fresher knew that the mention of money would more than likely get the young lady's attention. He recalled those days getting his Masters and PhD were lean times.

Fresher was right. Carol Lee quickly put a smile on her face and invited the two men to sit down.

"Please call me Carol."

As they took chairs across from the young lady, Fresher brought out the copy of the book and slid it across the table. She took it and began to leaf through the pages.

"Did you want me to read it to you, or actually write it out in English?"

"Well, writing it out would be great. How long will it take?"

"There are only a few dozen pages so perhaps an hour or so. Do you want to wait?"

"No, we'll grab a coffee and come back."

"Before you go, would fifty dollars be okay?"

"Yes, Carol. That would be more than acceptable."

An hour later, the three sat at the table. Ms. Lee was clutching her hand written notes and was visibly upset. Her face was pale and she sat staring at the two men.

"Dr. Fresher, is this a joke?"

"No Carol, it isn't. Why?"

"Dr. Fresher, if what is written in this book is true, you must call the police immediately."

Both men looked startled. Cody reached out and took the copy of the book and her notes.

"Carol, I don't understand," Fresher said. "What could be that serious?"

"Read it for yourself. I want no part of this." Lee started to rise.

"Please Carol. Can you give us a quick overview of the book before you go? Besides I owe you fifty dollars." Fresher asked.

Tying to maintain some kind of composure, Lee sat back down, took a few deep breaths and began.

"Here is the short version. From what I can understand, the book belonged to a man named Jung Kwan. The first half of the book is a detailed description of the training exercises of the Princess Pats Canadian Light Infantry at Canadian Forces Base Wainwright in Alberta. The second half of the book looks like messages that Kwan sent to a person named Tia Wang in Seoul, Korea. There are two messages, very detailed that describe the size of the Canadian force as well as the tactics that would be used in two upcoming invasions. The first is Operation Killer in February 1951 and the second Operation Kaypong in April 1951. These operations were supposed to take Hills 419 and 677 respectively. The next few pages look like messages back to Kwan confirming that the Chinese lost both battles, but significant damage was done and the Canadians impeded just long enough to give the Chinese time to prepare for the Battle of Hook."

Cody interrupted. "Harold, I know about these operations and battles from my research. The Battle of Hook was a critical engagement for the allies."

"Carol, is there more?" Fresher asked.

"Yes, there is also a page of ledger entries. Given that the initials 'SW' and 'JO' are listed, it's pretty obvious that the two names on the inside back, Jason Oliver and Stanley Ward, are those two people. The page lists credits and debits but the total debits do not add up to the total credits. I am not an accountant but it seems to me that the one named Jung Kwan kept some money for himself."

Still visibly shaken, Lee sat with her eyes wide open staring at Cody.

"Ms. Lee, do you recognize the name Tai Wang?"

"No, I haven't heard her name before."

"Her?"

"Yes, Tai is a woman's name."

"Carol you have been extremely helpful. We are asking that you keep this information confidential until I can get back to you. It might be a week or so, but I will be in touch. Please, can I have a contact number for you? Here is one hundred dollars."

"But I thought fifty dollars was what we agreed on?"

"It was, but the extra fifty is for being so helpful and your silence."

****

Back at the hotel, Fresher and Cody sat over a large lunch in Fresher's room and tried to make sense out of what they heard from Carol Lee. Fresher smiled looking at Cody eating as if John hadn't eaten in a few weeks. Good, he thought, John Cody needed to be healthy when he was reunited with Pamela.

Throughout lunch, the two men discussed what they now knew. No doubt the book appeared to be a record of espionage and payments. A person named Jung Kwan played a critical role. How Young got it, why he kept it, and why it was so important to him were still mysteries.

"John, you mentioned that you read about the Battle of Hook. What was that?"

For the next several minutes, Cody explained the significance of Hook. It was a crescent-shaped ridge that was strategically important to the Chinese Communist and the North Korean Armies. There were four battles for the ridge over a three year period. Prior to the first battle of Hook, the Princess Pats Canadian Light Infantry led in Operation Killer and Operation Kapyong. These battles were Canada's greatest. Both victories paved the way for the first Battle of Hook.

"Harold, I can see exactly what Kwan and his group did. They slowed PPCLI's down. Maybe we should take Carol's advice and go to the authorities."

Fresher sat back and slowly nodded his head back and forth.

"No, there is more, much more to this book than we know."

"What are you thinking?"

Fresher stood up and stared out the window for a minute before he turned to Cody.

"John, do you think that Kwan could be Young and that is why he wants the book back so badly. If that is true, the information in the book would destroy him. According to the original newspaper article that your step mother shared with me, he was 43 years old when you stole the book. That means that Young would only be 65 today with a lot of his life ahead. The others mentioned in the book probably don't even know that he kept the book or that they may be implicated. So on one hand he needs the book back to avoid it falling into the wrong hands and on the other, the people mentioned in the book pose a threat to him."

"That does make sense Harold."

"John, I think we need to look into Young's background but we'll need to wait until Monday."

****

The two men spent Sunday talking about Fresher's background and education and a few of the unique cases that Fresher had in the past couple of years.

"Harold, I am beginning to feel like I'm in jail again. Is there any chance that I could go for a walk?"

"I need some fresh air too. Let's slide down to the pier. It'll be cool, but if you are in Halifax, you shouldn't miss it."

Mid morning Monday, Fresher picked up the phone and made a call to Paul Parker, deputy police chief in Calgary.

"Hi Paul, Harold Fresher again."

"Dr. Fresher, twice in a few days, it must be some case you are working on. Is it still the missing man in Hamilton?"

"Yes I am still on the same case but I found him. He isn't back in Hamilton but he isn't missing anymore."

"So if you found him, then what can I do for you?"

"Paul, I have a story that you need to hear. It's a story that could have a significant impact on Harry Young and involve the armed forces."

"You mean the same Harry Young that was robbed way back?"

"Yes, the same."

Fresher spent the next fifteen minutes sharing information gathered over the past few days. He told him about Cody's involvement starting with his real name, the adoption, the robbery and prison and the transition back to his birth name. He explained that Cody took a small book during the robbery, hid it in Cold Lake just before his arrest and it was recently recovered intact. The book has been translated from Chinese to English and he knew why Cody was in danger, in danger from Harry Young. He left the theory to the end.

"Paul, the book centres on espionage against the Princess Pats Canadian Light Infantry in 1951. We know that Kwan Jung is the author of the book and I think that Harry Young may really be Kwan Jung."

"Stop right there Dr. Fresher. If there is any hint of espionage, you must send me the book so I can involve the RCMP."

"I agree that the RCMP should eventually become involved, but I need to make sure my theories are correct so that my client is not in danger."

"What do you need?"

"I need to know about Young's background including where he emigrated from, his immigration documentation, his jobs, anything. If he is

Kwan Jung, his arrest and conviction will bring relief for my client and his family."

"Dr. Fresher, I will help, but whatever I find, I need your assurance that the book comes to me before you do anything."

"I have nothing planned. Yes, I'll get the book to you very soon."

****

"Harold, I had the feeling when you were talking to the policeman in Calgary that you had something in mind."

"You're very perceptive John. Before we knew what was in the book, I thought that a simple plan may be best. I would contact Young and act as intermediary. In exchange for the book, Young would forget Harris Simons forever. Now, that isn't what might be best. The information that Ms. Lee provided has added a new level of complexity that implicated people in some espionage and I now think that we wait until we see what information Parker comes up with."

Chapter 10

Over lunch, Fresher pushed Cody.

"John, why didn't you just tell Pamela about your past? You knew she would find out one day."

"I should have, but she is a rare woman, one that I never thought would love a man like me if she knew."

Before the conversation could continue, the phone rang. It was Samid.

"Harold, Paul Parker wants you to give him a call."

"When did he call Samid?"

"A few minutes ago."

Just as he was pulling the receiver away from his ear, he heard Samid.

"Harold, Harold, there was one other message. It was from a woman named Jenn Gallager. She wanted me to remind you that your stitches should come out. She left her number."

Fresher smiled and rubbed the stitch-less cut on his left hand. She will be surprised when he tells her how they were removed.

Fresher quickly dialled Paul Parker's number.

"Hello Paul, Harold Fresher here."

"Dr. Fresher, you may want to sit down."

Fresher could sense the anxiety in Parker's voice.

"Go on Paul."

Parker went on to tell Fresher that Harry Young had emigrated from Beijing with his sister, Han in 1948. Young's immigration papers were under the name Jung Kwan, born July 6, 1923. His occupation was listed as pipe fitter so the Canadian Government shipped him to Alberta thinking that he could be an asset in the oil fields.

"Paul, is there any information after his immigration?"

"Nothing in that file, but I was able to find out that Kwan didn't take a job in the oil fields, rather he worked as a janitor at Canadian Forces Base Wainwright in 1948. The Base was still very active and just started housing the Princess Pats Canadian Light Infantry that were training and eventually deployed to Pusan, Korea. He stayed there until the end of 1951 when the base was winding down. He moved to Calgary, bought a small convenience store and called it Young's Flower and Groceries. It looked as if it was at that time he went from Jung Kwan to Harry Young. Within five to six years, he owned a string of these stores across Alberta and British Columbia. He married June Wong in 1958 and the next time there was any information was the robbery. That's about it."

"Thanks Paul."

"Dr. Fresher, you were right. Kwan is Young. So now that you know, I need that book as quickly as possible."

"Paul, I'll get it to you as soon as I get back to my office."

****

"John, you need to stay here for a few more days. I have to get back to my office today. I will extend the room and here is some money. Please stay in the room as much as you can and don't make any calls."

Fresher was on an evening flight thanks to a short stand-by list.

The next morning Fresher was in his office early and Samid was already there. His first concern was the book.

"Samid, did the book arrive?"

"Yes, it's in the safe."

Samid gave him two telephone messages from Pamela Cody. He knew that he couldn't tell all, but he owed it to her to give her some hope.

"Samid, please call Mrs. Cody and ask if she can drop in later today. Also, here is the name and number for a Carol Lee at Dalhousie. Can you try and get her on the phone. Whoever answers, tell them it's urgent."

Fresher retrieved the photocopy of the book and laid it on his desk. He knew that he was in possession of proof in espionage but the safety of John Cody was still foremost in his mind. As he sat behind his desk, he unconsciously put his hand in his pocket and felt the patterned cloth from the book. He pulled it out and after a brief look at it, put it back in his pocket.

After a five minute wait, Samid had Carol Lee on the phone.

"Hello?"

"Ms. Lee, Dr. Fresher here."

"Hello Dr. Fresher. Have you gotten any closer to solving your mystery?"

Lee sounded a lot less alarmed about the book's contents since they left her.

"You are very perceptive. I don't recall me telling you that I had a mystery to solve, but now that you have mentioned it, yes, I do have a mystery on my hands."

"Where are you in terms of getting a solution?"

"This is highly confidential, but I can tell you that I have involved the authorities."

He didn't exactly mean the RCMP, but he talked to Paul Parker at the Calgary Police Force. A small lie, he thought.

"That's good."

"Carol I'm sending you another $100 asking that you continue to keep our work in a highly confidential manner. Everything will unfold soon and you will understand the outcome."

"You can count on me Dr. Fresher."

"Thank you. By the way Carol, is there a more convenient phone number where I can reach you?"

"Yes. If I am not in the library or class, I'm at home."

Fresher jotted her number down and thanked her before hanging up.

Pamela Cody arrived at 11:30 that morning.

"Pamela, please have a seat and let me pour you a coffee. I need to tell you something before you ask me any questions."

Pamela Cody sat on the edge of her seat holding her coffee with both hands. Her tired red eyes were riveted on Fresher.

"I have been with John for the past few days."

Pamela Cody's eyes widened and she immediately started with the questions.

"Where is he? Is he alright? When can I see him?"

"Slow down Pamela and let me explain. He found me. You told him that you hired me and he got in touch. He did the right thing for himself and for you. I can't tell you where he is, but I will tell you that he is well, has enough money for another week or so and that I may be able to get him back to you soon. The case is quite complex and there is an element of danger in it, and I believe that there is a way to get all of us to a positive end."

Pamela Cody stared at Fresher.

"How ... when ... will he be okay? What can I do?"

"I mentioned the danger aspect. Is there anyone you can trust your business with for a week?"

"Yes. Whenever John and I did have a chance to get away, our backup dispatcher runs the operation. I could always catch up on the finances when I return."

"Okay. I want you to take a trip for a few days. I need you out of touch. I will explain all of this when you get back. Wherever you wind up staying, call Samid and give him a contact number."

Pamela Cody got up and walked over to Fresher giving him a hug before leaving his office.

It was now just after noon and as soon as Pamela Cody left, Fresher made another call to Parker.

"Hi Paul."

Parker wasted no time asking Fresher if the book was sent to him yet.

"Soon, but first you need to hear the entire story."

"Dr. Fresher, this is serious. The information is incredible and I need to bring Young in now."

"Paul, please listen to a story about this book first."

Fresher took the next half hour relating how Harris Simons, the same Harris Simons that he asked Parker about a few days ago, inadvertently took a small notebook during the Young robbery. Before his arrest in Cold Lake, Simons wrapped the book in a plastic garbage bag and hid it. Recently, the book was recovered and Fresher had it interpreted. It was in Chinese, and was a clear case of espionage during the Korean War. CFB Wainwright and the Princess Pats Canadian Light Infantry were targets of that espionage. The book noted others, one of which was probably in Korea. He went on to tell Parker that his client, Harris Simons was now John Cody and he was in danger.

"Dr. Fresher, this is a national security issue as well as a local police problem. We can protect Harris, Cody, or whatever his name is. I want that book as soon as possible."

"Yes, you are right, but I need one more thing first. Can you see if your files have anything on Jason Oliver, Stanley Ward, or Tai Wang?"

A few minutes later, Parker came back to the phone.

"We have nothing on Tai Wang. There is a Jason Oliver in our files. He is a local banker living a very respectable life in the community. He even supports our Policemen's Ball. Stanley Ward had a few run-ins with us, mostly drunk and disorderly. He passed away in 1981. I also looked at

Harry Young a bit closer. Young is one of the jewels in the community. He is a very successful business man who hosts many charity events and is one if the residents that is the salt of the city. I'll fax the files to you if you want."

"Thanks Paul. What did Ward do for a living?"

"According to our files, he was a retired communications technician for the Army."

"Paul, I am asking for a very, very big favour. Is there any way that you will trust me for another day before I courier the book to you?"

There was a long silence before Parker answered.

"Dr. Fresher, I can't. If I don't have the book Wednesday afternoon, I am going to the RCMP with what you told me."

"Paul, I hear you. If I get the book to you by tomorrow afternoon, will you give me another twenty four hours before you act?"

After another long silence, Parker responded. "It's a deal Dr. Fresher, but that book must be here."

"I owe you hugely. Next time I am in Calgary, we can do Caesar's Steakhouse, on me."

"Dr. Fresher, remember, tomorrow afternoon at the latest."

Fresher knew that Parker wouldn't act until he had the book in his hand and he would have to have it interpreted by his own people just to make sure that the information Fresher gave him was correct. But once that happened, word would spread fast and who knows what kind of danger Cody would be in from Young's cronies that would surely have connections in the Police Department. He also knew that the RCMP was not quick to move on a case that may implicate a foreign government so John Cody would remain in danger for some time.

It was time to take a real step out of the box and timing would be everything.

"Samid, can you pull out the black book from the safe and send it overnight courier to Paul Parker at the Calgary Police Department."

Securing express courier delivery, Samid sent the book to Paul Parker so he would have it by Wednesday late afternoon. The package had a note reminding Parker of the agreement and to wait until after 6:00 p.m. Thursday before going after Young and Oliver. Fresher said that he needed the time to secure safety for his client and his family.

****

The fax from Calgary arrived shortly after four o'clock. He started with Jason Oliver.

Jason Oliver, born in Edmonton in 1925. Public and High School in Edmonton. Graduated University of Calgary 1944 with a degree in Commerce. Worked as an accountant for Lowell Associates, a small Calgary firm until 1946 when the economy was picking up after the war. Hired by the Bank of Western Alberta and sent to CFB Wainwright to establish a store front bank for the soldiers and their families. Transferred to Calgary in 1952. Rose up the ladder reaching Senior Manager of Consumer Banking in 1982. Lowell Associates recruited him back as Senior Manager of Commercial Banking. Personal life included married to Helen in 1945. Deceased 1952. Married Loretta in 1953. Three children. Lived on Chestnut St. since 1953. Declared net worth of $1.4 million.

Fresher immediately saw the connection. All three men had been at CFB Wainwright in 1951. Was it possible that Ward sent the information to Tai Wang through his communication channels? Was it possible that Oliver was the banker laundering money from Tai Wang for Young's information?

Fresher arrived at the Hamilton Library a few minutes before closing and opened the Calgary yellow pages quickly finding Lowell Associates. Their half page advertisement promoted international accounting expertise, with a focus on the Asian markets. Fresher reread Oliver's information and tried to establish his role. He worked for Lowell just as the world war two ended so any travel by Oliver to Asia would have been out of the question. He married a woman named Helen in 1945 who died a year after he was transferred back to Calgary. The dates reflected that she was with him when he was at CFB Wainwright. Something wasn't right. If the book had Oliver's and Ward's name in it, why wouldn't Helen be in there as well? It would have been impossible to keep their activities from her.

Fresher located the first payphone and called Ms. Lee's residence hoping she was there. After all, by Fresher's calculations, it was seven o'clock in Halifax.

"Hello Ms. Lee, its Dr. Fresher. I wanted to thank you again for all your help."

"No problem. I am happy that the matter has been given to the authorities."

"Yes, I expect that we will know the outcome quite soon. Ms. Lee, I was wondering if the name Helen had a Chinese equivalent."

"Han."

"Han? Did you say Han?"

"Yes."

Fresher saw it all come together. Oliver's first wife was Young's sister. There was no doubt in Fresher's mind that the ring of conspirators included Young, Young's sister, Oliver and Ward, and Tai Wang in Korea.

He sat in the payphone booth having put it all together but knowing that John Cody's safety was still his first concern.

Fresher was exhausted and picked up a sandwich before heading home for a night in his own bed. As he finished his tea, he looked down at the uncovered scar, picked up the phone and called the number that Jenn Gallager left. The call went to voice mail and Fresher contemplated hanging up. Instead, when he heard the beep, he said, "Hi Jenn. It's Harold Fresher. Thanks for the reminder about the stitches. I had them removed and it is a story you will enjoy. Hope to chat with you soon."

Chapter 11

The following morning, Fresher was up early and in his office before Samid. It was Wednesday already and he knew that if the book wasn't to Parker by close of business that day, he would be damaging a helpful relationship, extending Cody's danger as well as affecting his own reputation. His first task was to share as much contact information about Young and Oliver with Samid and ask that he get both home and office numbers for each.

Fresher had a rough plan and it included needing to bring them out into the open. He knew that Young was a man with patience and was still eager to get the book back and obviously kept connections on the wrong side of the law as he was able to reach into a federal penitentiary and pay for the safety of Cody. Any attempt to broker a deal for the book that would release John Cody from Young's retaliation could not even be contemplated. Young wasn't to be trusted. Oliver was still a bit of an unknown, but if he helped Young in 1951, he could be capable of anything.

Fresher spent the rest of the day working out the details of his plan including a script of exactly what he would say to each man.

As Fresher was preparing to leave the office, Paul Parker called.

"Dr. Fresher, I received the package and have sent it to our translation team. It isn't that I don't trust your interpreter but if this ever goes to court, the department needs to have their creditable people involved.

"I understand Paul. When do you think you will get it back?"

"I expect it late this afternoon."

"You saw my note?"

"Yes, but after 6:00 tonight you can be sure that if the information is confirmed by the interpreters, I'll be making arrests."

"Trust me Paul. My client will be safe and you will have these two on a silver platter."

"Dr. Fresher, what do you mean, 'have these two on a silver platter'?"

"I'm asking you to trust me."

"Okay, 6:00 but not a minute later."

****

At four thirty Calgary time, Fresher made the first call from a phone booth at a nearby hotel lobby. He couldn't chance his name coming up on call display.

After two rings, a voice came on the phone. "Lowell Associates. May I help you?"

"Mr. Oliver please."

"I'm sorry Mr. Oliver is in a meeting. May I take a message?"

"This is the hospital calling and I need to speak to Mr. Oliver now."

In an anxious voice, the receptionist said, "Please hold. I will get him immediately."

A few minutes passed when Fresher heard a man's voice on the phone.

"Oliver here. What is this all about? Is someone hurt?"

"I am someone interested in Harry Young, or should I say Jung Kwan, your brother-in-law."

There was a long silence.

"Mr. Oliver, are you still there?"

Another long silence.

"Yes, I am still here. What do you want?"

"It turns out that your name was in a book he kept in his safe that implicated you to espionage that occurred during the Korean War. Kwan and his sister Han, and a man named Stanley Ward spied in 1951on the Princess Pats Canadian Light Infantry and fed it to a woman named Tai Wang in Korea. You were the banker at CFB Wainwright and acted as the broker to ensure that you four were paid. The book was stolen several years ago and Young doesn't know where it is"

"Who is this?"

"Someone who wants to see justice done."

"What do you want?"

"Go to the RCMP and tell them the story."

"You must be kidding."

Fresher hung up and sat back and smiled. He then picked up the phone and called Harry Young.

Fresher was surprised that Young answered the phone.

"Harry Young."

"Mr. Young, or should I call you Mr. Kwan, I just spoke to Jason Oliver."

Again, silence.

"Who is this?"

"As I said, I just spoke to Jason Oliver. I think you may remember him as your brother-in-law. Did you call her Helen or Han? Anyway, you were at CFB Wainwright with him in 1951. Stanley Ward was working with the three of you and was sending communications regarding the Princess Pats Canadian Light Infantry to a woman named Tai Wang in Korea. That information was used against Canadian forces to allow the Chinese army to get a foothold in preparation for the Battle of Hook. Oliver was your banker. He knows you lost the book, the book with all the details and names in it. "

In a very irritated voice, Young responded. "Is that you Simons?"

"No I am not Harris Simons, but I have the book and I'm much more dangerous than him. Goodbye."

"No wait. What do you want? Can we negotiate for the book?"

"Go to the RCMP and tell them the story."

"I cannot do that."

Fresher hung up. The rest was up to human nature.

****

As soon as Young hung up, his phone rang. It was Oliver.

"Young, what did you do? You kept a diary and then lost it?"

"Oliver. We have to meet."

Within half an hour, the two old accomplices sat in a dark corner of a bar across town, a bar that either would not have gone into if it wasn't an emergency. The tension between the two men was obvious.

"Young you fool, why did you keep a diary?"

"Don't call me a fool Oliver. Don't forget who master minded that job. You should be happy that it provided a nest egg for your future not to speak of the longer range business arrangement that we have. What I did or did not do is my business. The question we have is who has the book and where it is."

"At least you can tell me what happened."

Over the next few minutes, Young described the robbery and the book being taken. He told of Simon's prison time, his protection, and the unexplained disappearance. A man named Levitch was involved and he wasn't any help. The next thing that Young heard was the call earlier that evening.

"Look Young, you need to find that book."

"Oliver, before you go, are our other books safe?"

"Don't worry."

The two men left the bar and headed home. As both pulled up to their respective driveway shortly after six that evening, the Calgary Police accompanied by the RCMP were waiting for them with search warrants in hand. Young and Oliver were arrested.

****

The next day, Parker called Fresher at eight in the morning.

"Dr. Fresher, I thought I would give you a quick call and let you know what went down last night."

"Paul, it must be six in the morning there."

"Yes, I have been up all night but it was well worth it thanks to you."

"No, thank you Paul. I needed the extra time not just for my client but also to make sure that Young and Oliver would be rattled and wouldn't slip away. So what happened?"

"Well, the first part is that a story regarding the arrest of Young and Oliver for espionage will break in tomorrow's paper. The RCMP is including Army Intelligence going forward."

"You said first part. Is there a second part?"

"This part is highly confidential Dr. Fresher but you deserve to know what we discovered as a result of your work. During the search of both premises, we were looking for any additional incriminating information regarding what happened in 1951. What we weren't expecting was to find two more books, finance registries, in Oliver's house. I can't understand why Oliver wouldn't have kept those registers in a safe deposit box rather than in his desk at home. Those registries were a mother lode of information - names, dates, amounts - implicating Oliver as a money launderer for the Triple Union Society, better known as the Chinese mafia. You can guess who Oliver's contact was - Young. The RCMP was working with various authorities around the world for the past few years trying to get this specific information on this group. I was told this morning that the information in the two registries goes deep into the Society, perhaps one of the largest networks of organized counterfeiters and drug traffickers in the world. The RCMP is in round up mode and once they find and arrest others, they will press charges and let the courts take over."

"Paul, that is incredible."

"Dr. Fresher, I am assuming that the missing Hamilton man will be reunited with his family."

"Yes, Paul. Now that you gave me the news of the arrest, it will be my first order of business today."

"Dr. Fresher, the RCMP wanted to know who sent me Young's note book."

"I don't have to tell you that the Triple Union Society is lethal when it comes to interfering with their operation. Is there any way that you can keep Cody and me out of this?"

"I already have. I told the RCMP that it was received anonymously. I don't think they believed me, but they have a much bigger case now and don't seem interested in pursuing any link between Young's note book from almost thirty years ago and registries involving the Society. Once the roundup begins, it won't take the Society long to figure out where the RCMP got their information. Young and Oliver have been placed in protective custody given that there is probably already a price on their heads."

"Thank you Paul. I appreciate the information and keeping us out of this. Hope we can see each other soon."

****

Fresher made two calls. The first was to John Cody in Halifax to come home as soon as possible. All was well and he would explain later. Cody cried as he hung up the phone.

His second call was to Pamela Cody telling her that John and she were now safe and he was on his way home. Pamela Cody sobbed as she said goodbye.

Calgary Gazette

Friday January 27, 1989

Jason Oliver a prominent Calgary banker and local businessman Harry Young were arrested Thursday evening at their homes. A source at the Calgary Police Department said that a combined RCMP-Police team acted on a tip from the public that Oliver and Young were conspirators in leaking valuable information regarding the Princess Pats Canadian Light Infantry missions during the Korean War to the Chinese in 1951. Young, also known as Jung Kwan, his sister Han, now deceased, Stanley Ward, also deceased, and Oliver worked at CFB Wainwright and had fed information to a Chinese contact in Seoul Korea. Oliver and Young are being held without bail and will be arraigned tomorrow.

There was no mention of the Triple Union Society, but then again, Parker told Fresher that this would only be the first part of the story unfolding.

****

On Saturday January 28, Fresher sat with John and Pamela Cody in their front room enjoying a coffee. Pamela bought Sumatra blend to serve Fresher. She sat legs tucked under her on the couch holding on to John with both hands and all her might. It was clear that they were in love and would never part. He gave them a copy of the Calgary Gazette article and filled in the blanks such as how Paul Parker helped uncover the story. Fresher and John Cody reminisced about Carol Lee's involvement and Pamela Cody suggested that she receive another 'thank you' payment. They all laughed, but it was a nervous laugh.

"Harold, what do you think will happen now?"

"My best guess is that because the charge is espionage, they will be held in custody until the crown has prepared the case. This could take four to six months or even longer. They won't get bail because it is so serious. It actually carries a life sentence."

"Can Young or Oliver ever get to John?"

"That would be the very least of their concerns Pamela. What I just found yesterday was that a search warrant for Oliver's house turned up information that implicates Young and a number of people in organized crimes not only across Canada but offshore as well. Oliver and Young will become very unpopular for losing these records. Nobody now cares about the book you stole.. Frankly, I wouldn't give Oliver and Young much chance of surviving prison. I find it ironic that both kept records that eventually destroyed them. Fools books, wouldn't you say?"

Pamela and John Cody relaxed for the first time in several months.

John Cody kissed Pamela's hand tenderly.

"Pamela, I need to tell you something."

For the next half hour, he told the whole story, his story - the armed robbery, prison, his birth mother, the change in identity, Levitch's accidental meeting - all of it. Pamela looked lovingly at her husband and reached out for him giving him a hug with both arms tightly around his heck. Fresher saw the tenderness in their relationship. They both turned to Fresher.

"Harold, I am not sure how I will ever be able to repay you for what you have done not just for me, but for us."

"Speaking of payment, I think there is a few hundred dollars left in your account with me. I'll get that to you in a week."

"No, Harold", she said with a smile. "Please keep it. It will buy Sumatra for a while."

Fresher asked, "John, what are you going to do about Levitch? He has your ten thousand."

"Knowing him, that money is long gone and I really don't want to ever see him again. I need to concentrate on replacing the money I took from our account and speak with Pamela's family. They deserve to know the truth and to be thanked for helping us out. I also need to arrange for my mother to meet Pamela."

"John, I was glad to be able to help. Now, I'm off to my office to catch up on a backlog of cases. Take care."

Pamela and John Cody got up from the couch and went to Fresher. There were no handshakes only hugs.

****

Without the traffic of cars and people, downtown Hamilton in winter was quiet on Saturdays and even though he was still tired from the Cody case, he went through messages in his office. He made a fresh pot of Sumatra coffee sifting through the paper on his desk and reflecting on the Cody's. He smiled thinking that some stories do have very happy endings.

Just then Samid came in.

"Harold, what brings you in here today?"

"The same as you...work. Is the Cody case wrapped up?"

Fresher told Samid the entire story and explained that the left over retainer money was a bonus. He told Samid to take fifty dollars and enjoy a good dinner that night.

Samid left the office just after noon hour leaving Fresher alone in the quiet. The scar on his left hand was itchy and reminded him of Jenn. 'No time like the present', he thought.

He dialled her number expecting to leave a message but was startled when she answered the phone."

"Hello."

"Jenn, its Harold Fresher."

"Harold. I got your message. How is the hand?"

"Just like new."

"Good."

"How is the case going?"

"Wrapped up yesterday."

"That's good. You must be exhausted."

"Nothing a couple of days of rest won't cure."

There was an awkward silence for a few seconds.

"Harold, are you free tonight? I won two tickets to a new play at the Centre."

Without any hesitation he replied, "Yes, I would enjoy that, and I will treat to a late dinner. What is name of the play?"

"It's called, 'Little Black Book'. Apparently it's a comedy."

"Are you kidding?

"No, why?"

"I'll fill you in at dinner."

****

A light snow had started and by the time that Fresher and Gallager left the theatre, the city looked like a winter wonderland. He drove to a casual Italian restaurant that catered to the late night crowd. Gallager was shocked when he told her how he had the stitches removed. She immediately took his left hand and inspected the scar smiling with approval. Fresher took a few minutes and gave her the reason he was so startled when she told him the name of the play. The dinner was full of laughs and the meal was excellent including a bottle of Amarone.

"Jenn, I can't remember an evening I enjoyed more. Thank you for inviting me to the play."

She reached across the table and put her hand over his.

The waiter brought the bill to the table. As Fresher pulled out his money, the square gold cloth with gold dots was stuck to his money clip. He picked it up and went to place it in the ashtray when Gallager stopped him.

"Harold, where did you get this?"

"Why?"

"It has an interesting importance to the Chinese."

"I thought it was filler under the liner of the book. What is so important about it?"

"Red and gold are considered good luck."

Fresher smiled knowing that it wasn't good luck for Harry Young, but on the other hand, it brought him good luck as far as Jenn Gallager was concerned.

"Harold, can we do this again?"

"Next weekend?"

Gallager smiled and nodded yes.

16520864R00080

Made in the USA
Middletown, DE
23 November 2018